A to Z of
CLASSIC
HOLLYWOOD
STYLE

A to Z of CLASSIC HOLLYWOOD STYLE

Compiled by

Sinty Stemp

Abrams / New York

Editor: Rebecca Kaplan
Designer: Here Design
Production Manager: Erin Vandeveer

Library of Congress Control Number: 2013935714

ISBN: 978-1-4197-0851-0

First published in 2012 by V&A Publishing
Victoria and Albert Museum
South Kensington
London SW7 2RL
www.vandabooks.com

Printed and bound in Hong Kong
10 9 8 7 6 5 4 3 2 1

THE ART OF BOOKS SINCE 1949

115 West 18th Street
New York, NY 10011
www.abramsbooks.com

INTRODUCTION

'Film . . . the most perfect visual medium for the exploitation of fashion and beauty that ever existed.'
James Laver, museum curator and art and fashion historian, 1899–1975

Long before Hollywood made stars, there were stars who made Hollywood: this 1967 tribute to actress and style diva Gloria Swanson sets the scene for *A to Z of Classic Hollywood Style*. Promoted by the all-powerful film studios and the moguls behind them, Hollywood's stars developed and presented their image with the help of costume designers who were often personally chosen. This pairing would be an ongoing partnership honed through a whole career, with costume designers and, sometimes, couturiers providing both on-screen and off-screen wardrobes for their stars. The relationship was intimate and important; it mattered as much to the smooth process of filming as to the eventual success of the film, and maintained a star's position in both the studio system and in the eyes of the film-going public. Star and costume designer were inextricably bound in a mutually enhancing relationship; its apogee from the 1930s to the 1950s, known as the Golden Age of Hollywood, when Hollywood increasingly called the glamour and style shots, and audiences and copyists lapped up what they saw on the silver screen— the choice of precious metals here, gold and silver, highlights the special place Hollywood style held in contemporary culture. A star was a star, off-screen and on-screen, promoted by famous stills photographers such as George Hurrell, Clarence Sinclair Bull and John Engstead, and a host of fan magazines. It was an all-encompassing occupation; as director George Cukor said of Joan Crawford, 'She was always "Joan Crawford, Star."'

The demise of the star/studio system in the 1960s brought about a generalized loss of glamour and ushered in a new sense of realism. The new generation of young stars had no time for the extended image-making that, for a previous generation, had defined Hollywood style. The 1960s mantra 'anything goes' extended to Hollywood's stars. The new crop of actresses was no longer interested in standing out as style legends; they were more interested in getting behind the camera and directing, rather than enhancing their style credentials in front of it.

In the past, Hollywood image was a valued, productive and candidly discussed topic; actors, actresses, directors and designers, many of whom were feisty and individual characters, were forthcoming and articulate on the subject. It is ironic but interesting that, despite the popular cult of celebrity style, modern Hollywood is surprisingly reticent on the subject and comparatively light on good quotes, but this is, in itself, a commentary of sorts. As critic Kenneth Tynan observed, 'I think the sensual side of acting is too often underrated: too much is written about how actors feel, too little about how they look.'

Today, Hollywood style is evoked largely off-screen, migrating from the production lots and stars' leisure time to the red carpet. Star style is now a more distanced affair, filtered through an entourage of stylists and publicists, hairdressers and makeup artists who, more or less, determine what a star will look like when they decide to dress up. Most often represented by paparazzi shots of stars in low-key casual dress, Hollywood style today is a more homogenous and less individual affair. Rather than stars setting style themselves through the alchemy of star and costume designer, just as the red carpet is the new venue for Hollywood style, so the designer catwalk defines and supplies it. Few stars stand out for their own singular and consistent sense of personal style. Even so, their red carpet forays are the exception rather than the style rule.

This collection takes a broad view of topics and Hollywood players, male and female, over a span of time. Inevitably, some subjects have had to be reluctantly omitted and some individuals make several appearances based on their impact, influence and iconic status. Chosen for their informative, often witty content, these mini-commentaries are acerbic, perceptive, revealing, celebratory, valedictory, pithy paeans to Hollywood style.

The image of the 'Divine' Garbo did not suffer from her trademark androgynous style; rather, her preference for an understated, mannish wardrobe played to her languid feminine magnetism (1931).

Accessories

The trend for naming handbags after female film stars began when French luxury firm Hermès renamed one of their styles the Kelly bag, after Princess Grace was featured on the cover of *Life* magazine in 1956 using hers to shield her pregnancy from the press. In 2005, British fashion designer Alexander McQueen named one of his first handbag designs the Novak, after Kim Novak, the cool blonde star of Alfred Hitchcock's *Vertigo* (1958).

'My hobbies in dress are shoes and hats. I've given more thought to them, studied them more carefully than I have my dresses because they *make* or *mar* an outfit.'
Joan Crawford, actress, 1931

'I dislike looking dressed. I distinctly dislike newness in clothing. I never wear a hat until I have battered it and crushed it so that it looks well worn and comfortable. The same with shoes.'
Fred Astaire, actor, dancer, choreographer and singer, 1899–1987

Age

'I believe in loyalty. When a woman reaches a certain age she likes, she should stick with it.'
Eva Gabor, actress, 1919–95

'I'm like fine wine. I get better with age. Now I'm more me than I ever was, so you get a bonus.'
Mae West, actress, playwright and screenwriter, 1893–1980

'Everyone grows older, except Cary Grant.'
Grace Kelly, actress, 1987

'When people tell you how young you look, they are really telling you how old you are.'
Cary Grant, actor, 1904–86

A

'Grant really had got better looking. The sensual lusciousness was burned off: age purified him (as it purified Paul Newman).'
Pauline Kael, American film critic, 1975

'Preserving what is left is more important than mourning what is lost.'
Cary Grant, actor, 1978

'Ava Gardner looked like a woman. She never tried to look like a girl . . . I like being a woman, not a girl.'
Sharon Stone, actress, 1958–

The American Silhouette

Joan Crawford's favourite costume designer, Adrian, promoted the shoulder-pad silhouette to slim her hips and accommodate Crawford's unusually broad shoulders. Although the look originated in the Paris couture collections, in France shoulder pads were known as *Americaines*.

Androgyny

'Greta Garbo is hermaphroditic, with the cold quality of a mermaid.'
Tennessee Williams, American playwright, 1911–83

'Deficient in all the surface frills of femininity, she [Garbo] replaced them with a male directness.'
Kenneth Tynan, British theatre critic and writer, 1954

'Greta Garbo always brought a spark that ignited everyone . . . She adored Reed [Diana Vreeland's husband], and Reed's overcoats. She'd walk up and down our apartment in Reed's overcoats, not to be admired but to enjoy being in them. She'd take one off and then she'd go into his closet and get into another one.'
Diana Vreeland, former fashion editor of Harper's Bazaar, editor-in-chief of American Vogue, fashion consultant to the Metropolitan Museum of Art and author, 1984

'I am, at heart, a gentleman.'
Marlene Dietrich, actress and singer, 1901–92

'Women's clothes take too much time—it is exhausting, shopping for them . . . Then the styles change—and it must all be done over again, every few months. It is very extravagant to dress as most women do. Men's clothes do not change; I can wear them as long as I like.'
Marlene Dietrich, actress and singer, 1933

'She has sex, but no particular gender. Her ways are mannish: the characters she plays loved power and wore slacks, and they never have headaches or hysterics . . . Dietrich's masculinity appeals to women, and her sexuality to men.'
Kenneth Tynan, British theatre critic and writer, 1953

'I am sincere in my preference for men's clothes—I do not wear them to be sensational . . . I think I am much more alluring in these clothes.'
Marlene Dietrich, actress and singer, 1933

'A black dinner suit, trousers, dandy jacket, cummerbund, and white frilly shirt may not be the most feminine getup ever, but Marlene Dietrich always did very well in something similar, I remember.'
Felicity Green, doyenne British journalist, reviewing French designer Yves Saint Laurent's 'Le Smoking' look, inspired by Dietrich's chic androgyny, 1966

Anglophile Style

'He dressed like an English gentleman.'
Leslie Caron, actress and dancer, on actor and dancer Fred Astaire, who successfully melded the casual and the elegant, 1988

'There was a whole set of people in New York who were really under the influence of the Duke of Windsor—the way they dressed, the elegance, the spiffiness, pressed pleats, casual, easy. They were all friends of his, and I think they brought that style to Hollywood. Hollywood didn't really have that kind of elegance until this whole group of people moved out there—the Gershwins, my dad [director, Vincente Minnelli], Fred Astaire, Vernon Duke, Cole Porter.'

Liza Minnelli, actress and singer, 1988

'He was wonderfully elegant, an Anglophile, always very smart. Grey flannel trousers and tweed coats.'

Jeremy Tree, British racehorse trainer and friend of Fred Astaire's, 1988

'Fred had a great knack for dressing, a flair—not gaudy, just a touch. He used to have white shoes with black edges around the soles, which looked very chic. His ties were always the right colour, and his coats were never extreme. I think his whole style was English. He used to get his clothes made at [Savile Row tailors] Anderson and Sheppard. Sometimes the movie people would wonder if he didn't look too English; they wondered if they shouldn't Americanize him a little.'

Hermes Pan, Fred Astaire's choreographer, 1988

Anti-fashion

'I care nothing about clothes . . . When I am off the set I don't want to have to think of clothes at all. I like to live simply, dress simply.'

Greta Garbo, actress, 1905–90

'If it is true (as I think it is) that none of Garbo's clothes ever appear to be meant for her, much less to fit her, that is because her real state is not in clothes at all. Her costumes hamper her . . . She implies a nakedness which is bodily as well as spiritual.'

Kenneth Tynan, British theatre critic and writer, 1954

'The whole concept of fashion freedom began with her.'

Women's Wear Daily, on Greta Garbo, attributed

'Garbo has been credited with having little clothes sense and obviously pays no attention whatsoever to the rules of current fashion . . . If she is unwilling to devote her time to becoming a well-dressed woman, she has succeeded, nevertheless, in creating a fashion for herself and, though nonconformist, has been an important factor in contributing to the tone of a whole period.'
Cecil Beaton, photographer, designer, artist, writer, close friend, admirer and reputed lover of Garbo's, 1954

'If she [Garbo] liked a thing, she wore it with complete unconsciousness. No matter how eccentric it was, she gave it an air of authority.'
Adrian, costume designer, quoted by Hollywood gossip columnist and actress Hedda Hopper, 1952

'No star was ever more obviously dressed-up in the clotheshorse sense, or less obviously so in the social sense . . . the most luscious siren of all resented her furbelows, preferring to go about like a lady golfer after a hard afternoon.'
Parker Tyler, American film critic, comments on the contrast between Garbo's on- and-off screen wardrobes, 1963

Attention-seeking
'Conspicuousness is the unforgivable sin in the art of dressing.'
Travis Banton, costume designer, 1894–1958

'I believe it's better to be looked over than it is to be overlooked.'
Mae West, actress, playwright and screenwriter, 1893–1980

'She dressed to excite attention; hers was a more sumptuous, more theatrical, more striking look.'
Edith Head, costume designer, on actress and singer Marlene Dietrich, 1959

'I like to be really dressed up or really undressed. I don't bother with anything in between.'
Marilyn Monroe, actress, 1926–62

Under Hitchcock's direction and in Edith Head's costumes, Grace Kelly's brief film career nevertheless established her as Hitchcock's ideal blonde, beautiful and beautifully dressed (1955).

Beauty

'Without security, it is difficult for a woman to look or feel beautiful.'
Merle Oberon, actress and famed beauty, 1911–79

'If you aren't pretty, make no attempt to be pretty. Be smart like Frenchwomen.'
Adrian, costume designer, 1903–59

'Miss Garbo is not a conventional beauty, yet she makes all other beauties seem a little obvious.'
Harriette Underhill, American film critic, 1926

'There is no personal achievement in being born beautiful.'
Loretta Young, actress, 1913–2000

'Pastel prettiness has never appealed to me, only vital beauty. The born beauty's perfection has a tiresome sameness while the attractive woman must work at it, making the most of each good point.'
Joan Crawford, actress, 1930

'Ah, this is real beauty. We blondes have to work for it.'
Marlene Dietrich, 1901–92, actress and singer, on actress and renowned beauty Dolores del Río

'Better legs than Dietrich and better cheekbones than Garbo.'
A critic's verdict on actress Dolores del Río, attributed

'Take care of your inner spiritual beauty, and that will reflect in your face. We have the face we created over the years. Every bad deed and fault will show on your face. God gives us beauty, and genes give us our features; whether that beauty remains is determined by our thoughts and deeds.'

Dolores del Río, actress who reputedly owed her flawless complexion to a regime including orchid petals and up to sixteen hours of sleep of a day, 1905–83

'I always notice a woman's complexion first. I think it's the most important feature. You can't be beautiful without beautiful skin. There's no way to look young if your skin gets old.'

Mae West, actress, playwright and screenwriter, 1893–1980

'Marilyn's principal asset was her translucent white luminous skin. Her skin was pneumatic; one could almost touch it on screen. Cineastes refer to this phenomenon as "Flesh Impact."'

Eve Arnold, American photographer, on Marilyn Monroe, 1987

'[The camera is] the first engine for imposing types of beauty . . . one curious result of the power of the film has been the spread of type-consciousness to classes which have previously known nothing of such conceptions. Every important film star appeared in *Vogue* and contributed some new look or fashion:

Garbo—hollowed eye sockets and plucked eyebrows

Dietrich—plucked eyebrows and sucked-in cheeks

Joan Crawford—the bow-tie mouth

Tallulah Bankhead—a sullen expression

Mae West—the hourglass figure and an attractive bawdiness

Constance Bennett—a glazed bandbox smartness

Jean Harlow—platinum hair

Katharine Hepburn—red hair and freckles

Vivien Leigh—gypsy colouring, a glittering combination of white skin, green eyes and dark red hair.'

James Laver, fashion historian, museum curator and writer, 1899–1975

'The most incredible face ever seen by man. No makeup—unmatched beauty.'
Lauren Bacall, actress, on screen legend Greta Garbo, 1978

'[The screen's] most classic beauty.'
Sir Winston Churchill, 1874–1965, British politician and former Prime Minister, on actress Elizabeth Taylor

'[Audrey Hepburn] . . . today's wonder girl. She has so captured the public imagination and the mood of the time that she has established a new standard of beauty, and every other face now approximates to the "Hepburn look" . . . This slim little person, with the winged eyebrows and Nefertiti head and throat, is the world's darling.'
British Vogue, 1954

'Audrey gave beauty a new concept. Movie stars in the 1950s looked like Lana Turner and Ava Gardner. Then along came this waif-like creature with these doe eyes.'
Roger Moore, actor, 1999

'I'd like to be beautiful but sometimes I think I am strangely put together . . . They always write about me as the girl with the Fu Manchu fingernails and the nose as long as an anteater's.'
Barbra Streisand, singer and actress, 1966

'Style is more interesting to me than beauty. Style is about panache and about embracing individuality . . . that's what beauty is about for me—celebrating uniqueness not conformity.'
Isabella Rossellini, actress and daughter of actress Ingrid Bergman, 1997

'Nothing makes a woman more beautiful than the belief that she is beautiful. Beauty is how you feel inside, and it reflects in your eyes. It is not something physical.'
Sophia Loren, Italian actress and voluptuous beauty, 1934–

'Beauty to me is about being comfortable in your own skin. That, or a kick-ass red lipstick.'
Gwyneth Paltrow, actress, 2008

Best-Dressed Lists

The annual International Best-Dressed List, or BDL, a list of the world's most stylish women, voted for by industry insiders and society figures, was popularized by American fashion publicist Eleanor Lambert: grande dame of fashion arbiters. She compiled the lists from 1940 until her retirement in 2000 (a men's list was added from 1966), and the tradition continues, notably in *Vogue*, *Vanity Fair* and *Harper's Bazaar*.

'A well-dressed woman, even though her purse is painfully empty, can conquer the world.'
Louise Brooks, actress, dancer and writer, 1906–85

'The youngest Impeccable is film star Audrey Hepburn, who is also the youngest to be enshrined in the BDL Hall of Fame . . . She is the one movie star with high fashion taste, which is completely removed from Hollywood low taste.'
John Fairchild, publisher and author, 1965

'He had it, that's all. He had something that few men have—he was not just the best dressed, but he had a manner of wearing his clothes as though he had no clothes on at all. They seemed just accidental. He had an ease, a perfection that was just marvellous. I don't think he ever had any idea that he was setting a style. It was just how he liked to look. He used that look in films a lot . . . He was always the best casually dressed man.'
Nancy 'Slim' Keith, Lady Keith, American socialite, on Fred Astaire, 1988

'The best-dressed man of our time—the strongest influence of freestyle elegance in the twentieth century.'
The International Best-Dressed List citation for Fred Astaire, 1979

'The carefree, the best-dressed, the debonair Astaire! What a myth! My hats are too small, my coats are too short, my walk is too loose.'
Fred Astaire, actor, dancer, choreographer and singer, 1960

'Still the most handsome, the most elegant, the best dressed, the best taste, the best of everything of anybody I've ever worked with, male or female. I can say nothing more flattering.'
Edith Head, costume designer, on debonair actor Cary Grant, 1975

'Greta Garbo, the greatest actress the screen has given us, was the worst dressed woman in the world.'
Coco Chanel, Paris couturière and fashion designer, 1883–1971

Bias Cut

The technique of cutting fabric on the diagonal, pioneered by Paris couturière Madeleine Vionnet (1876–1975) in the 1920s, creating what American journalist Virginia T. Lane called 'that intriguing slinky look' in 1932.

'The Girl Who Made the Bias Line Famous.'
Hollywood label for actress Jean Harlow, 1932

'[White] 60-inch [angelskin] satin is a favourite for these slinky dresses because it lends itself to an unbroken line in cutting, doing away with seams, from bust to hemline.'
Jean Harlow, actress who owned an original Vionnet bias-cut dress, on her screen wear, 1932

'Those beautiful clinging clothes that Jean Harlow wore—that was sex.'
Edith Head, costume designer, 1983

'After I got the role of Bonnie, Arthur Penn and I started talking about what she might wear. I thought jeans, maybe pants of some sort since they were robbing banks . . . But Warren [Beatty] and Arthur wanted to put her in dresses, great costumes that would give her style . . . The look for Bonnie was smack out of the 1930s, but glamorized and very beautiful . . . They were all cut on a bias and they swung.'
Faye Dunaway, actress, on her Bonnie and Clyde *(1967) costumes, 1995*

'On the bias, fabric becomes much more difficult to handle because it has its own way of wanting to fall. But if you understand how it will fall, you can create with it. The fabric subtly leans into the body, and is very aware of who is wearing the cloth. It's a very sexy look.'
William Travilla, costume designer, 1920–90, who combined the bias cut with sunray pleats for two of Marilyn Monroe's most famous looks: her gold lamé halter-neck dress in Gentlemen Prefer Blondes *(1953), and her white halter-neck dress in* The Seven Year Itch *(1955)*

Blondes

In 1995, Canadian anthropologist Grant McCracken devised a 'blondeness periodic table,' divided into six categories, with different aspects of blonde appeal defined by Hollywood stars: the 'bombshell blonde' (Mae West, Marilyn Monroe), the 'sunny blonde' (Doris Day, Goldie Hawn), the 'brassy blonde' (Candice Bergen), the 'dangerous blonde' (Sharon Stone), the 'society blonde' and the 'cool blonde' (Marlene Dietrich, Grace Kelly).

'I like to feel blonde all over.'
Marilyn Monroe, in response to being asked why she didn't tan

'No one ever sounded as blonde as Marilyn Monroe did.'
Billy Wilder, director and screenwriter, 1999

'It takes a smart brunette to play a dumb blonde.'

Marilyn Monroe, actress, original brunette and iconic platinum blonde, 1926–62

'It is possible that blondes also prefer gentlemen.'

Mamie Van Doren, American actress and pinup, 1931–

'Blondes are the best victims. They're like virgin snow which shows up the bloody footprints.'

Alfred Hitchcock, director, 1973

Bond Girls

'I think, obviously, at that time Ursula [Andress]'s whole look was very different from women that had come before. It was a very athletic, very strong, physical look. She meant business, and she is so stunningly beautiful.'

Barbara Broccoli, producer, on the quintessential Bond girl: Ursula Andress as bikini-clad Honey Ryder in Dr. No *(1962), 2003*

'It's a mystery. All I did was wear this bikini in *Dr. No*, not even a small one, and Whoosh! Overnight I have made it.'

Ursula Andress, actress who reputedly designed the bikini that made her an international sensation while dramatically increasing sales of bikinis worldwide, 1964

Steve McQueen's own laid-back, casual way of dressing created a new Hollywood male figurehead, equally attractive to men and women, and earned him the title 'King of Cool' (1968).

Censorship

'[Under the mechanism of the Hays Office Production Code of 1930] There were strict rules decreeing exactly how much of the body could be exposed. In the 1940s, the emphasis on bosoms of the time and the amount of cleavage permitted was left to the discretion of a man from the censorship office, whose okay was necessary for every dress and costume before it could be shot. [I was] on set when a censor was on the job, a small grey man, serious and stern at his job; he stood in front of Lana Turner's well-padded bosom, peering down her low-cut dress. Shaking his head, he turned to the designer standing anxiously beside him and said, "You'd better cover the cleavage with net or tulle. It'll never pass the office."'
Irene Sharaff, costume designer, 1976

'When I was eighteen in Hollywood, the wardrobe lady had to measure my cleavage. Only one and a half or two inches were permissible exposure. If too much was showing, in went a disgusting flower.'
Joan Collins, actress, 1978

'I love to do the things the censors won't pass.'
Marilyn Monroe, actress, 1926–62

Charisma

'She is one of a selected few who aren't actors by our standards, but if you put them on the screen they emanate something—something I frankly don't understand. Brando has it, Monty Clift used to have it and, of course, Garbo had it.'
Richard Burton, actor, on actress Elizabeth Taylor, whom he married twice; together they were a famously charismatic couple, 1963

'She seemed to have a kind of unconscious glow about her physical self that was innocent, like a child . . . She enjoyed it without being egotistical.'
Elizabeth Taylor, 1932–2011, actress, on fellow actress Marilyn Monroe

'A star is someone who creates atmosphere around himself, a personal magnetism that is controversial, that is loved, or hated. Someone who has glamour and talent to give to the world and does it unreservedly, without inhibition, and does it in spite of himself.'

Luis Estévez, Cuban-born fashion and costume designer, 1965

'She's five feet four inches but she looks six feet on the screen.'

Steven Spielberg, director, on screen icon Joan Crawford, 1995

'There was such an aura about us that we would have shone just as brightly even without the diamonds and the pearls.'
Lana Turner, actress, 1983

'What makes a star? Everything! Charisma—what I used to call in drama school "the shine." Internal, emotional, physical energy—it goes beyond the body and you can't control it.'
Faye Dunaway, actress, 1989

Classic Style

'It is a mistake to have extreme fashions, for they will date a film. Often films appear old because of their clothes, though they are quite modern in ideas. The dress designer must foresee the trend of fashions to come and give the clothes that classic touch which makes them last as long as required for the exhibition of the film. Also, the film has such a wide public appeal that it influences fashion all over the world. A glamorous film star's lead is sure to be followed, so it is doubly important that film clothes should be in good taste.'
Elsa Schiaparelli, couturière and sometime costume designer for Hollywood actresses, among them Mae West and Zsa Zsa Gabor, 1934

'Hitchcock made everybody in the picture dress in a classic style . . . He didn't want the picture to date because of the clothes. There's not one outfit I couldn't wear today with a few minor adjustments and not look stylish.'
Eva Marie Saint, actress, on her wardrobe for North by Northwest *(1959), personally chosen for her by Hitchcock, 2006*

'If you look at Cary Grant's suits from the 1930s, '40s and '50s, they still look good today. That's style, not fashion.'
Glenn O'Brien, magazine editor, columnist and style writer, 2000

'I don't dress for the moment.'
Cary Grant, actor, renowned for his timeless style, 1904–86

Cleavage

'Adrian's focusing on the shoulders was gradually replaced by a new concentration on the bosom. When I started to work in Hollywood, there was no star or starlet who did not know the exact size of the padding she thought she needed in her bra to be sexy. The word "sexy" was synonymous with the size of the bosom. One result was that most of the young actresses clamoured for more and more padding and ended up looking as though they were supporting the Himalayas across the chest.'
Irene Sharaff, costume designer, 1976

'What the good Lord has forgotten, we'll put there with cotton.'
Mae West, actress, playwright and screenwriter, advice to the less well endowed, 1893–1980

'They spend a long time worrying about whether a girl has cleavage or not. It seems to me, they ought to worry if she doesn't have any.'
Marilyn Monroe, actress, 1926–62

'She may single-handedly make bazooms a thing of the past.'
Billy Wilder, director and screenwriter, on Audrey Hepburn, the antithesis of the curvy Hollywood pinup, 1999

'For *Star Wars* (1977), they had me tape down my breasts because there are no breasts in space.'
Carrie Fisher, actress and author, 1983

C

Colour

'Every woman has weapons. One of them is colour: colour not only can change the way a woman looks, it can change the way she feels, the way she thinks.'

Edith Head, costume designer, 1959

'I've been identified with pink throughout my career, but I'm not as crazy about it as I've led people to believe. My favourite colours are actually neutrals—black and white—but then who thinks of a movie queen in black and white? Everything has to be in living colour.'

Jayne Mansfield, actress and sex symbol, 1933–67

'Personally, I'm loyal to blue, black and white. Very bright shades seem blatant and harsh to me on the street. I invariably want to turn and walk in the opposite direction from them. They are like harsh, discordant voices.'

Joan Crawford, actress, 1931

'Make me a dress with myriads of ostrich feathers . . . a blue dress, like the blue you find in the paintings of Monet.'

Ginger Rogers's instruction to costume designer Bernard Newman, on her dress for the dance sequence 'Cheek to Cheek' in the film Top Hat, *1935*

'It's really very simple, Edith. Keep the colours quiet, unless we need some dramatic impact.'

Alfred Hitchcock, director who meticulously plotted costume in his film direction, to costume designer Edith Head, 1959

'Unless there is a story reason for a colour, we keep the colours muted because Hitchcock believes they can detract from an important scene. He uses colour actually almost like an artist, preferring soft greens and cool colours for certain moods.'

Edith Head, costume designer, on Hitchcock's treatment of colour as more than mere scenery, 1978

'This week has been a swine . . . So many unexpected snags cropped up . . . Eliza [Doolittle]'s ascot appearance gave me a nasty jolt. The scarlet poppies on her hat became orange. But who would have guessed that in the long shots the black and white striped lacings and bows would appear green and yellow? I was very distressed, and Carol, who made the dress, said that when she heard the news she had to take a couple of aspirin. Audrey [Hepburn], to comfort us, told of how they had to discard a zebra coat, made by Givenchy, in her last film, as that photographed bright yellow.'
Cecil Beaton, photographer, designer, artist and writer, 1964

'His marvellously sure sense of colour put life on the screen. His red coats, apple-green costumes, or the dress in shocking pink have never been forgotten by cinemagoers.'
Audrey Hepburn, actress, on Parisian couturier Hubert de Givenchy, 1990

Colour Coordination

Joan Crawford coordinated the fabric covers of her vodka flask with her outfits. When Cary Grant's hair lightened to grey, so often did his suit colour.

'He [Cary Grant] has the greatest fashion sense of any actor I've ever worked with. He knows as much about women's clothes as he does about men's. When we were making *To Catch a Thief* (1955), he planned a colour scheme for his wardrobe throughout the picture. He found out what Grace Kelly was wearing in each scene, then selected clothes to complement hers.'
Edith Head, costume designer, 1959

'Never were there two more opposite performers in a film than Joan Crawford and Bette Davis. On the day we made our tests for [*Whatever Happened to Baby Jane?*] (1962), Joan came to my dressing room and said, "I do hope my colour scheme won't interfere with yours." "Colour scheme??? Joan, I haven't a speck of colour in any dress I wear. Wear any colour you want. Besides, it is a black-and-white film."'
Bette Davis, actress, 1987

Cool

'Men still respond to his style in those films.'

Theadora Van Runkle, costume designer who sealed Steve McQueen's sartorial cool credentials by putting him in Savile Row suits for The Thomas Crown Affair *(1968) and well-cut casual separates and aviator sunglasses for* Bullitt *(1968), 2010*

'You can't put a guy in a black suit without him looking a little cooler than he already looks.'

Quentin Tarantino, director, producer, screenwriter and actor, whose film, Reservoir Dogs *(1992), was notable for the stylish black-suit wardrobe of its male stars, 1993*

'An icon of eccentric cool—offbeat and idiosyncratic.'

GQ on actor Johnny Depp, voted Most Stylish Man in the World, 2010

Costume Design

'You could line up all the gowns and tell the screen story.'

Adrian, costume designer, 1903–59

'A clever designer can substitute costume for whole scenes through the mere expedient of making clothes talk . . . It is sketching a character by virtue of scissors, needle [and] thread.'

Adrian, costume designer, 1934

'My job was to change people into something they weren't—it was a cross between camouflage and magic.'

Edith Head, costume designer, 1978

'[A costume designer is ideally] a combination of psychiatrist, artist, fashion designer, dressmaker, pincushion, historian, nursemaid and purchasing agent.'

Edith Head, costume designer, 1959

'Drape the body rather than squeeze it into forms of distortion.'
Orry-Kelly, costume designer on films including Casablanca *(1942) and* Some Like It Hot *(1959), 1897–1964*

'He wanted her to look like a piece of Dresden china, something slightly untouchable.'
Edith Head, costume designer, on Alfred Hitchcock's look for Grace Kelly's fashionable character in Rear Window *(1954), 1983*

'A designer is only as good as the star who wears their clothes.'
Edith Head, costume designer, 1959

'He's famous for Dietrich's costumes, even though I do all the work. You don't make a dress for Dietrich, you make it with her.'
Marlene Dietrich, actress and singer, on her favourite costume designer, Travis Banton, 1976

'Then [the 1930s], a designer was as important as a star. When you said Garbo, you thought of Adrian; when you said Dietrich, you thought Banton. The magic of an Adrian or Banton dress was part of the selling of a picture. Sets, costumes, and makeup just aren't considered the art forms they used to be.'
Edith Head, costume designer, 1959

'I depend on Givenchy in the same way that American women depend on their psychiatrists.'
Audrey Hepburn, actress, on couturier and friend Hubert de Givenchy, 1969

'Now the stars of the screen have shirts that seem to be glued to their backs, or a simple dress. I mean, what happened to those films where the actresses had at least twenty costume changes?'
Valentino, Italian couturier and fashion designer, 2009

· C

Couturiers in Hollywood

'Her dresses weren't sensational enough. She made a lady look like a lady. Hollywood wants a lady to look like two ladies!'

The New Yorker's verdict on Chanel's chic but understated costumes for glamour queen actress Gloria Swanson in Tonight or Never, *1931*

'The most elegant Chanel dress of the early 1920s was a washout on the screen. When you strip colour and sound and the third dimension from a moving object, you have to make up for it with dramatic black-and-white contrasts and enriched surfaces.'

Howard Greer, costume designer, on Chanel's short-lived stint as a Hollywood costume designer, 1949

Couturiers on Hollywood

'Before motion pictures, the public never anticipated Paris. We could hold a style for six months or a year with perfect safety. Today, however, you are putting so many pretty gowns in your American pictures, striving so hard to make your pictures novel in their costumes, that we must keep on the alert to stay ahead of you!'

Paul Poiret, Paris couturier, on Adrian's designs, having visited the set of Madam Satan, *1930*

'We, the couturiers, can no longer live without the cinema any more than the cinema can live without us. We corroborate each other's instinct.'

Lucien Lelong, Paris couturier, 1935

'Cinema is life. I want to stay in the moment.'

Elsa Schiaparelli, couturière, 1931

'Cinema has had the same effect on fashion as the atomic bomb; the ratio of the explosion of the moving image throughout cinemas knows no bounds on Earth.'

Coco Chanel, Paris couturière, c.1945

C

'What Hollywood designs today, you will be wearing tomorrow.'
Elsa Schiaparelli, couturière, 1890–1973

'It is through the cinema that fashion can impose itself today.'
Coco Chanel, Paris couturière, 1931

'I, who admire American films, am still waiting for studios to impose a figure, a colour, a style of clothing. Hollywood can deal successfully with the face, with the outline, the hairstyle, the hands, the toenails, with portable bars and refrigerators in the drawing room, clock radios, with all man's repercussions and knickknacks, but it doesn't deal any more successfully with the central problem of the body, which it has not managed to disassociate from man's inner drama, and which remains the prerogative of the great designers and ancient civilizations. At least until now.'
Coco Chanel, Paris couturière, c.1945

Cravats

A favourite accessory for Hollywood's best-dressed and most debonair matinee idols, when casually dressed still meant dressing up sufficiently, among them Errol Flynn, Fred Astaire and Cary Grant. For Grant, the cravat and neckerchief also represented camouflage. Due to his earlier Vaudeville career as an acrobat and juggler, Grant had developed a thick-set neck, which he disguised by having the collars of his handmade shirts cut higher. In Hitchcock's *To Catch a Thief* (1955), the French Riviera setting required a more casual daytime wardrobe, so a series of cravats and neckerchiefs were used to camouflage his neck.

Drama Hollywood-style: actress Dolores del Río shows how the simplest outfit can be the most dramatic and enhancing through the use of clean, sculpted lines and well-placed details (1933).

Décolletage

'Low necklines stylish? They're imperative!'
Mae West, actress, playwright and screenwriter, 1893–1980

'Must I always wear a low-cut dress to be important?'
Jean Harlow, actress famous for wearing revealing dresses, 1911–37

'I have always liked wearing clothes up to my throat . . . Adrian . . . went to great lengths to help me avoid anything too low-cut.'
Greta Garbo, actress, 1905–90

The Importance of Detail

'Queen Dietrich is the perfectionist. No hook or eye, no seam is unimportant. Crews may falter, fitters faint, designers contemplate hara-kiri; Dietrich remains indefatigable, and each detail must be right. Once it's right, it can be better . . . What's more, she knows . . . Dietrich was born knowing.'
Edith Head, costume designer, 1959

'I'd rather know that the seams of my stockings are straight than wear diamonds.'
Joan Crawford, actress, 1931

'It takes five hundred small details to add up to one favourable impression.'
Cary Grant, actor, 1977

Divas

'It is sad that nowadays, true divas are so very rare. There's Liz Taylor, Sophia Loren, but the list is short. Even a remarkable actress cannot really be considered a diva in the sense once attributed to the term: [today] when she leaves the set, where she has perhaps worn sumptuous outfits, she wears a T-shirt and jeans, she steps out of the "dream." It is a pity so few [Hollywood] people nowadays pay attention to style.'
Valentino, Italian couturier and fashion designer, 2009

Drama

'The dramatic situations in a picture must be costumed according to the feeling of a scene . . . A jeweller, you know, shows his finest diamonds on a plain bit of black velvet, not on a gorgeous piece of metallic embroidery.'
Adrian, costume designer, 1926

'Few people in an audience watching a great screen production realize the importance of any gown worn by the feminine star. They may notice that it is attractive, that they would like to have it copied, that it is becoming, but the fact that it was definitely planned to mirror some definite mood, to be as much a part as the lines or the scenery, seldom occurs to them. But that most assuredly is true.'
Adrian, costume designer, 1903–59

'As a rule, clothes should serve as a background and not attract any special attention to themselves, but sometimes they must have the opposite effect: emphasize the character of the wearer and take on a special dramatic quality.'
Travis Banton, costume designer, 1938

'In *The Birds* (1963), the fashion was not too important; once we established Tippi Hedren's character was a well-dressed woman, Hitchcock preferred that the audience not notice her clothes. He didn't want any distractions from the terror.'
Edith Head, costume designer, 1959

Dresses

'Dresses! I wish they were all bags, and all alike to jump into quick!'
Greta Garbo, actress, 1931

'Say what you want about long dresses, but they cover a multitude of shins.'
Mae West, actress and inveterate long dress wearer, 1893–1980

'The right dress makes life an adventure; the wrong one makes it a dull bore.'
Joan Crawford, actress, 1905–77

'The right dress can triumph over any situation, build any mood, create any illusion, and make any woman into the sort of person which she most desires to be.'
Norma Shearer, actress, 1934

'You can have everything you want in life if you dress for it.'
Edith Head, costume designer, 1897–1981

'Wearing the correct dress for any occasion is a matter of good manners.'
Loretta Young, actress, 1913–2000

'Our interest was in making the star attractive [rather] than making an attractive dress. That is the difference. In couture, it is to make the dress look beautiful and sell. In pictures, it was to make the star look the way she should.'
Edith Head, costume designer, 1959

'A woman's dress should be like a barbed-wire fence: serving its purpose without obstructing the view.'
Sophia Loren, Italian actress and beauty, 1934–

'Where women are concerned, the rule is never to go out with anyone better dressed than you.'
John Malkovich, actor, 1953–

'I dress for women and I undress for men.'
Angie Dickinson, actress, 1931

'Behind every successful man you'll find a woman—who has nothing to wear.'
James Stewart, actor, 1990

Dietrich's Rules for Dressing on a Budget

Despite her couture wardrobe and legendary status, Marlene Dietrich retained a down-to-earth perspective. Her rules on frugal dressing are practical and still relevant today.

'Don't ever follow the latest trend, because in a short time you will look ridiculous. Don't buy green, red or any other flamboyant colour dress. A small wardrobe must consist of outfits you can wear again and again. Therefore, black, navy blue and grey are your favourite colours. Don't buy separates. Don't believe the sales talk that you can have five dresses for the price of one. And don't buy cheap materials, no matter how attractive the dress looks to you. Don't say you can't afford a dress made of expensive materials. Save up for it. If you have one good suit, preferably grey (navy blue gets shiny), two black dresses, a black wool skirt, a couple of black and grey sweaters, you'll be well dressed most of the year until summer, when you'll wear simple cotton dresses. Another suggestion, don't send your clothes to the cleaners all the time. Spot-clean and press them yourself. It's worth it because they last longer. And while you're saving up for that good black dress, on your next date wear a black sweater and skirt. Nothing wrong with that as long as you don't ruin the elegance of the outfit by overemphasis of the bosom.'
Marlene Dietrich, actress and singer, 1961

'Emphasis above the table': Costume designer Adrian's graphic sequin- and bead-embroidered design focuses attention on Katharine Hepburn's expressive face and sculpted features (1940).

Elegance

'Rarely found today. Women are not brought up to know about it and therefore lack even the desire to acquire it.'

Marlene Dietrich, actress and singer, 1961

'Her [Carole Lombard's] clothes always looked as if they belonged to her. Some girls never learn to wear elegance naturally, but it seemed that Carole had always known how.'

Edith Head, costume designer, 1959

'[Dolores del Río] has that rare quality of elegance, which many seek but few find. I do not know quite how to say it, but it is a quality that lends distinction to anything she wears, and gives to the dress or hat a part of her own personality.'

Lilly Daché, milliner, 1946

'What is poignant about Marilyn is that, all her life, she wanted to be a lady. Elegance [to her] was elusive, fearful, attractive and awesome . . . Miss Monroe, having her voluptuous figure and no neck, was not free of the desire to be elegant. In fact, I think it was a major force in her life, a true source of motivation.'

Norman Mailer, American writer, 1980

'Besides being absolutely beautiful, Grace [Kelly] had an elegance that never went away.'

Albert Wolsky, American costume designer, 1930–

'A woman of elegance will never cease to surprise you.'

Alfred Hitchcock, director, 1962

'Fred Astaire: Elegant! Elegant! Elegant!'

Marlene Dietrich, actress and singer, 1961

'Fred Astaire's achievement—no, his glory—was that he made elegance infectious. He democratized and Americanized the word most overused to describe himself.'
Richard Schickel, American writer, journalist and film critic, 1987

'The elegance of the old days is gone.'
Cary Grant, actor, on his reason for retirement, 1966

'Emphasis Above the Table'

Acknowledging the frequency and dramatic importance of close-ups and medium-range shots in cinematography, the Hollywood costume designer Adrian's maxim 'Emphasis above the table' ensured that his designs for female Hollywood stars focused attention on the top half of the body, accentuating the face and neckline through the use of sequin and bead embroidery, graphic monochromatic contrasts, extravagant collars and bows.

'The most important shots were the close-ups: clothes were most often seen from the waist up, and that's where you had to concentrate; an elegantly detailed skirt was almost superfluous.'
Oleg Cassini, fashion and costume designer, 1987

Eyelashes and Eyebrows

By a natural but unusual mutation, Greta Garbo and Elizabeth Taylor were blessed with a double set of upper eyelashes. False eyelashes were a Hollywood innovation, achieving wider popularity via endorsement by its stars, both on- and off-screen.

'She has natural eyelashes more lovely than any artificial lashes I can supply.'
Max Factor, cosmetician, on Greta Garbo, 1926

'Such a profile, such grace, such poise, and most of all, such eyelashes. They swish the air at least a half-inch beyond her languid orbs.'
Harriette Underhill, film critic, on Greta Garbo, 1926

'Who has double eyelashes except a girl who was absolutely born to be on the big screen?'
Roddy McDowell, actor, 1928–98, on his friend and costar, actress Elizabeth Taylor

'The reduction of the eyebrow to a minimum presence and the lifting of lid and eyelash to a maximum presence was first a Garbo trait. The Joan Crawfords and the rest came afterward.'
Parker Tyler, American film critic, 1963

'Instead of eyebrows, she has limned butterflies' antennae on her forehead.'
Cecil Beaton, 1904–80, photographer, designer, artist and writer, on Marlene Dietrich's plucked eyebrows

'A mannequin . . . with eyebrows like African caterpillars.'
Bette Davis, 1908–89, actress, on rival actress Joan Crawford, who later in life sported a famously heavy style of eyebrow

E

Jean Harlow in Adrian's luxurious beaded satin negligée with 22-inch ostrich feather cuffs represents Hollywood's ultimate boudoir look and sheer escapism from the Depression (1933).

Fabrics

When talking films were introduced in 1927, microphone sensitivity picked up the rustle of stiff fabrics, distorting the sound quality. For their female stars, costume designers Travis Banton and Adrian were drawn to Vionnet's bias cut using fabrics (silk, crêpe, satin) that would mould to and skim over the body, a look that came to epitomize Hollywood's golden age of glamour.

'As the sense of luxury began more and more to depend on the confections of the movie imagination, colour drained out of elegance, and was replaced by the whole black-and-white spectrum. White gold and platinum came into vogue for jewellery and for hair; draped lamé and sequinned satin offered rivulets of light to the eye as they flowed and slithered over the shifting flanks and thighs of Garbo, Dietrich, Harlow and Lombard . . . For women's clothes, sequins, marabou, white net and black lace developed a fresh intensity of sexual meaning. [Mood] was transmitted through the behaviour, movement, and visual feel of fabrics instead of through colour; and this . . . lent itself very well to the new cool, self-sufficient female image.'
Anne Hollander, art historian and writer, 1978

Fashion

'Fashion is a language—some know it, some learn it, some never will. But Dietrich was born knowing it . . . Like all the fashion magazines in one, Dietrich's things were more than fashion—they were super fashion.'
Edith Head, costume designer, 1959

'We worked at choosing clothes in Paris . . . Dietrich was very selective. She did not shop around. She knew which designer suited the image and which would detract from it. So we only went to see the collections of Patou, Lanvin, Molyneux, and Madame Alix Grès. Not Chanel.'
Maria Riva, daughter and biographer of Marlene Dietrich, 1992

'I don't believe in following fashion—except when it suits you.'
Claudette Colbert, actress, 1903–96

'Never follow fads. There is a difference between novelty and originality. The former is for women who allow others to think for them. The latter is for those who think for themselves.'

Constance Bennett, actress, whose beauty and glamorous style made her a 1930s fashion pinup, 1904–65

F

'Don't follow [fashion] blindly into every dark alley. Always remember that you are not a model or mannequin for which the fashion is created.'
Marlene Dietrich, actress and singer, 1901–92

'A real star can start a fashion without knowing it and without anyone knowing why a fashion gets started in the first place . . . The great "stars" are not fashionable in the sense that they make a point of being well dressed. They dress instead for their personalities. Stars forget fashion and still set trends. Greta Garbo is badly dressed, but who cares? Garbo is way above fashion. She has survived all the other older stars and all fashions, and she still influences.'
John Fairchild, American publisher and author, 1965

'Joan Crawford and Carole Lombard were my style icons—I loved their clothes. The designers then were about what would look good onscreen—there was a marked difference between film fashions and street fashions that doesn't exist today.'
Julie Harris, British costume designer, 2010

Films That Influenced Fashion

Letty Lynton (1932): Joan Crawford's dramatic dresses; *Dinner at Eight* (1933): Jean Harlow's platinum blonde hair and slinky white satin gowns; *It Happened One Night* (1934): Clark Gable goes without a vest and causes a drop in sales of men's undershirts; *Gone with the Wind* (1939): nipped-in waists and a crinoline revival; *Roman Holiday* (1953): Audrey Hepburn's joie-de-vivre verve in jaunty neckerchiefs, full skirts and ballet flats; *The Wild One* (1953): leather biker jackets, boots, T-shirts and baker boy caps; *Rebel Without a Cause* (1955): teenage angst in jeans, T-shirt and windcheater jacket; *Breakfast at Tiffany's* (1961): showcases the little black dress, the ultimate in feminine chic; *Bonnie and Clyde* (1967): retro 1930s style brings hemlines down and knitwear in; *Doctor Zhivago* (1968): swaggering military coats and Russian bohemianism; *Love Story* (1970): Ali MacGraw's knitted beanie hat and scarf spark a trend; *The Great Gatsby*

(1974): ushers in drop-waisted dresses and a luxuriously pale palette; *Annie Hall* (1977): Diane Keaton's androgynous take on vintage menswear; *American Gigolo* (1980): sexy, sophisticated Italian tailoring, Armani-style; *Flashdance* (1983): dancewear and the customized sweatshirt take centre stage; *Out of Africa* (1985): a romanticized safari look; *Pulp Fiction* (1994): vampish bobbed hair, dark nail varnish and the white shirt.

'The nation is now burdened with snoods for women's hair as a result of the Scarlett and Melanie snoods. I assume you know that the costumes of *Gone with the Wind* (1939) are the basis of at least 50 per cent of fashions at this present moment, and I am sure the whole business of the return to corsets is due to [*Gone with the*] *Wind*.'
David O. Selznick, producer, 1939

'Joan Crawford in *Mildred Pierce* (1945) changed everyone's eye at the time with her clothes and styling in that movie. Her shoulders were bigger, her eyebrows bolder than anyone had seen . . . [Her look] had a graphic quality to it, and people thought it was a bit caricature. It wasn't until a little later that all that aggressive, bold attitude became really chic in a broad way.'
Isaac Mizrahi, fashion designer, 2011

'*Sabrina Fair* (1954), had made a huge impact on us all at [art] college; everyone walked around in black sloppy sweaters, suede low-cut flatties and gold-hoop earrings. Few of us, though, could imitate Audrey Hepburn's skinny elegance.'
Barbara Hulanicki, designer, 1983

'I love Spielberg and Scorsese, but they do not make the kind of film where the star "dictates" fashion. The style of Billy Wilder, for example, which was fantastic, no longer exists. Films like *Breakfast at Tiffany's* (1961) are no longer made, where the actress was identified with a certain outfit and everything revolved around the leading lady.'
Valentino, Italian couturier and fashion designer, 2009

'Givenchy, following his master Balenciaga, was the important forerunner of the minimalist designs of the 1960s. And [Audrey] Hepburn's films played a crucial role in changing sensibilities, so that by 1960, the 1950s stars seemed blowsy.'

Elizabeth Wilson, sociologist, academic and writer, 1993

'The Bonnie look became the rage . . . It was glamorized but real. The maxi replaced the mini of the 1960s because of this film. The clothing has the kind of classic lines that caught the imagination of European designers.'

Faye Dunaway, actress, on Theadora Van Runkle's 1930s-style outfits for Bonnie and Clyde *(1967), 1995*

Joan Crawford's Fashion Rules

'1. Find your own style and have the courage to stick to it.
2. Choose your clothes for your way of life.
3. Make your wardrobe as versatile as an actress. It should be able to play many roles.
4. Find your happiest colours—the ones that make you feel good.
5. Care for your clothes, like the good friends they are.'

Joan Crawford, actress, 1963

Feathers

'Ostrich plumes are popular, but they must be worn with discretion.'

Travis Banton, costume designer, 1894–1958

'I spent half my time at Cawston's Ostrich Farm in South Pasadena ordering ostrich feathers, riding in carts that were trundled about the place by trained ostriches.'

Edith Head, costume designer, on actress Mae West's predilection for ostrich feather trims, boas and fans for her film costumes, 1959

'I'm an actor. An actress is someone who wears boa feathers.'

Sigourney Weaver, actor, 1983

Femme Fatale

'[Travis] Banton spared nothing in dressing Dietrich. She was the femme fatale, and he used his couturier flair to define her character . . . Her trim silhouette allowed him to use thick, luxurious fabrics that would make most actresses look plump on screen. But not Dietrich. He could pin on ruffles, furs, and feathers and she always projected her svelte image.'

Edith Head, costume designer, 1983

Flapper Style

Charleston-dancing flappers epitomized the emancipated attitude to fashion, femininity and morality of the Roaring Twenties.

'Clara Bow is the quintessence of what the term 'flapper' signifies . . . pretty, impudent, superbly assured, as worldly-wise, briefly-clad and 'hard-berled' as possible.'

F. Scott Fitzgerald, American novelist and writer of Bernice Bobs Her Hair, *a short story about a would-be flapper, 1927*

'Joan Crawford, the best example of the flapper . . . gowned to the apex of sophistication.'

F. Scott Fitzgerald, American novelist and writer, 1927

'Something new has entered the world of clothes and personal adornment . . . It is the spirit of modernity. The spirit finds an expression in the clothes we wear. They are startling. They do not blend; they contrast. They do not rustle; they swing. They do not curve; they angle. Perhaps this new feeling in dress finds its first and most definite expression in the motion picture world. We are the first to exploit a style. The modern clothes spirit I am talking about is . . . the very essence of restless activity . . . the costumes are the costumes of my own personal wardrobe.'

Joan Crawford, actress, on the novelty of flapper style as exemplified by her role in the archetypal flapper film, Our Dancing Daughters (1928), 1928

Audrey Hepburn remains Hollywood's most famous gamine and gave this vulnerable, youthful and stylish look an eternal chic. Her aesthetic has been endlessly admired and emulated (1954).

Gamine

French term originally meaning street urchin or ragged child, applied to the slim, youthful looks and boyish cropped hairstyles of actresses such as Audrey Hepburn, Mia Farrow and, latterly, Selma Blair and Carey Mulligan.

'She was described as gamine, but for me, her charm lay not in the androgyny of simple hair and a boyish figure, but in a style that seemed the embodiment of sophisticated, existential Europe as opposed to the overripe artificiality of Hollywood.'
Elizabeth Wilson, British sociologist, academic and writer on Audrey Hepburn, 1993

Gangster Chic—Dressed to Kill

'At that time [1920s and '30s], the king thug on the Warner lot was Edward G. Robinson, wearing vast lapels like the swept-back wings of a jet.'
Kenneth Tynan, British theatre critic and writer, 1966

'Ever since *Public Enemy* in 1931, he had been Hollywood's most dynamic and disarming hood . . . He made vice look spunky and debonair.'
Kenneth Tynan, British film critic, on James Cagney, 1966

'George's suits were always the latest style. Wide lapels, wide trousers, spats, and you could cut your finger on the crease in George's pants. He was one of the first guys to wear a black shirt with a white tie. He wore long collars. A pearl-grey hat was pulled down over one eye. Come wintertime, he'd either be in a black form-fitted coat with a velvet collar or a sporty brown camel wraparound. He wore 50-buck shoes with pointy toes, shined so bright you could see your face in them.'
Mack Grey, actor, 1905–81, on actor, dancer and sharp dresser George Raft

'Gangsters are not only men of action, but also men of fashion, and the hat is essential to that image.'
Stella Bruzzi, academic and writer on film and television, 1997

Glamour

'Any girl can be glamorous. All you have to do is stand still and look stupid.'
Hedy Lamarr, actress, attributed, 1914–2000

'It was because of Garbo that I left MGM. In her last picture they wanted to make her a sweater girl, a real American type. I said, "When the glamour ends for Garbo, it also ends for me. She created a type. If you destroy that illusion, you destroy her." When Garbo walked out of the studio, glamour went with her, and so did I.'
Adrian, costume designer, 1903–59

'Glamour is what I sell, it's my stock-in-trade.'
Marlene Dietrich, actress and singer, 1901–92

'What Monroe is to sex, Dietrich is to glamour.'
Ray Jones, American photographer, 1900–75

'Glamour is just sex that got civilized.'
Dorothy Lamour, actress, 1914–96

'You can create glamour totally, I think. But a woman in our business generally has some quality of it. Some have it more than others. Joan Crawford, for instance, well, she projected that quality. Now, maybe it's because she thought in a sexy way . . . Rita [Hayworth], too. It was all instinct, and that comes across. It's alive. Harlow was another one like that. They were the products of that period; they thought that way, and they felt that way, they projected that quality. When they'd come through the door— they'd arrive somehow. They didn't just walk in saying, "Hello, how are you?" They'd develop that thing. You'd see them at cocktail parties, just idle things, but I never saw anything like it. When I think of it now, it seems humorous. It was as if they had internal trumpets that blew for them just as the door opens. Lana Turner used to do the same thing . . . but they all had it.'
George Hurrell, photographer, 1986

'You could feel an atmosphere to [glamour]. You felt inspired when someone like Dietrich or Crawford walked into the room. The real stars were conscious of glamour—that's part of what it meant to be professional.'
George Hurrell, photographer, 1986

'The word "glamour" means something indefinite, something inaccessible to normal women—an unreal paradise, desirable but basically out of reach.'
Marlene Dietrich, actress and singer, 1989

'Miss Crawford was a glamour puss; I was an actress.'
Bette Davis, actress, 1987

'Glamour! That's what the movie business is, isn't it? Yes, well, unfortunately, it isn't anymore. I've always said that glamour begins with cleanliness. Not makeup. Bathe first. That's number one with me. Glamour should never be superficial. It should be part of your habit, part of your lifestyle.'
Joan Crawford, actress, 1972

'Like charity, I believe glamour should begin at home.'
Loretta Young, actress, 1913–2000

'The catastrophe that the studios invited was the death of glamour, which had filled the air we breathed. The stars were asked to stop wearing the golden glow of gods and goddesses and look like plain folks . . . The geniuses who conduct the motion picture business killed glamour when they decided that what the public wanted was not dream stuff, but realism. They took the girls out of satin, chiffon, velvet and mink, put them first into gingham and then blue jeans.'
Hedda Hopper, Hollywood columnist and actress, 1963

'Once you're used to glamour, it's something you never want to be without.'
Lana Turner, actress, 1921–95

Gloves

'The Girl in White Gloves.'

Time magazine's moniker for Grace Kelly, 1955

'Grace [Kelly] got the same kind of joy collecting gloves as other women did diamonds . . . Gloves and shoes are the only things where Grace loses count of money.'

Edith Head, costume designer, who enjoyed shopping for costume accessories at Hermès with Grace Kelly, 1976

Gowns

'Above all, actresses are not mannequins displaying gowns. The gowns are to display actresses. A mannequin shows off the gown. A gown on the screen shows off the actress. And a gown must show off the specific actress who is wearing it. Gowns which fit their personalities, which fit the action of their pictures, which stand out or retreat according to the demands of that action. And gowns which can do all this, despite the loss of the value of colour and material.'

Gloria Swanson, actress, 1931

'The dress has to fit you mentally as well as physically. You must imbue the clothes with your own personality.'

Norma Shearer, actress, quoted by writer Robert LaVine, 1980

'I like gowns that are tight enough to show I'm a woman but loose enough to show I'm a lady.'

Mae West, actress, playwright and screenwriter, 1893–1980

Grace

'She was terrifically graceful, so all her movements were good, and that's something very important for the camera.'

Allan Dwan, American director on actress and dancer Rita Hayworth, 1977

'Grace Kelly was an ex-model, and she knew how to wear clothes. Every actress's contract should specify that she be trained in modelling or dancing, or at least go to school to learn how to wear clothes.'
Edith Head, costume designer, 1983

'Only Fred Astaire ever moved as well as Cary Grant, but Grant moved with more dramatic eloquence while Astaire cherished the purity of movement. Grant could look as elegant as Astaire, but he could manage to look clumsy without actually sacrificing balance or style.'
David Thomson, film critic and writer, 1982

'He walked with the threatening grace of a panther on the prowl.'
GQ quotes an observer on actor Sean Connery, 2010

'Slinky as a lynx, hot as pepper, cool as rain, dry as smoke.'
Ros Asquith, critic and artist, on actress Lauren Bacall, 1985

'She walks like a young antelope, and when she stands up, it's like a snake uncoiling.'
Jerry Wald, American producer and screenwriter on the young Marilyn Monroe, 1911–62

Grooming

'Any actress who appears in public without being well groomed is digging her own grave.'
Joan Crawford, actress, 1905–77

'She taught me to be immaculate, which is quite a different thing from being 'dressy.' I have never seen anyone more immaculate than Garbo. Her shining, brushed hair, her clean, strong hands, without nail polish or benefit of beauty parlour . . . She is so shiningly groomed that it makes all that seem cheap by comparison.'
Cecilia Parker, Garbo's costar in The Painted Veil *(1934), 1934*

'I no more think that you should use a lipstick, powder, deodorant or hairbrush in public than you would take a bath in public.'
Marilyn Monroe, actress, 1953

'There was something about [Cary] Grant that made his clothes stay in perfect shape. While on other people clothes developed stains, creases and spots, Grant's remained impeccable. Even his shoes never seemed to acquire scuff marks or the signs of wear.'
William D. Weaver, Cary Grant's assistant in the 1970s, 1987

'There was a translucent, pearl-like quality to her; everything about her was clear and fresh and fine—her skin, her scent, her hair.'
Oleg Cassini, fashion and costume designer on Grace Kelly, whom he almost married, 1989

'Beautifully groomed and casually tailored in her everyday wardrobe, Miss Kelly has influenced for the best the working-day costume of the average American girl.'
Cynthia Cabot, American journalist, 1955

'Off-screen [Kelly] was not the best-dressed actress in Hollywood, but she was always very fastidious about the way she looked. She wore white gloves and very sheer hose, and always carried a handkerchief. She was quite a contrast to the new stars.'
Edith Head, designer, 1983

'On the side starting to curve at the corner of my eyebrow and ending, sloping downward, at my cheekbone': 'The Wave,' Lauren Bacall's signature hairstyle, helped shape 'The Look' (1946).

Hair

Veronica Lake's blonde sweep of hair, cascading luxuriantly over one eye, known as the Peek-a-boo, was so influential in the 1940s that American government officials told the Hollywood actress to change it in case it caused accidents among female fans working with machinery on assembly lines in various war-work industries. Lake's response: 'Any girl who wears her hair over one eye is silly. I certainly don't, except in pictures'.

'[Louise Brooks] at 15, already a beauty, with her hair close-cropped at the nape, cascading in ebony bangs down the high, intelligent forehead and descending on either side of her eyes in spit curls slicked forward at the cheekbones, like a pair of enamelled parentheses.'
Kenneth Tynan, theatre critic and author, on the actress and Jazz Age flapper whose signature dark bobbed hair made her a style icon, 1979

'Few actresses have had their hair used so deliberately as a sexual metaphor. It might have escaped the watchdogs on the censor board, but audiences had no such problem.'
John Kobal, film historian and writer, on Rita Hayworth, 1977

'I am my hair.'
Rita Hayworth, actress, famed for her role as a redhead femme fatale in Gilda *(1946), 1992*

'I think the most important thing a woman can have, next to her talent, is her hairdresser.'
Joan Collins, British actress, 1933–

Hats

One of America's most talented milliners was John P. John, otherwise known as Mr. John, who collaborated with costume designers to create many of Hollywood's most memorable hats: from Garbo's *Mata Hari* (1931) jewelled skullcap and Dietrich's *Shanghai Express* (1932) feathered cloche to Vivien Leigh's Scarlett O'Hara picture hats and was consulted by Cecil Beaton on the design of Audrey Hepburn's *My Fair Lady* (1964) Ascot concoction.

'She wears hats with everything except her nightgowns.'
Edith Head, costume designer, on actress Gloria Swanson, 1959

'Hats can set a personality, establish a mode . . . Nobody thinks of Carmen Miranda without a tall turban loaded with flowers, fruit, beads and bangles . . . Usually I restrain myself a little. But with Carmen, the more fantastic fruits and birds and strange beads I could get together on one turban, the better.'
Lilly Daché, milliner, 1946

'Givenchy's hats! They always made the face appear in close-ups like a wonderfully framed picture.'
Audrey Hepburn, actress, 1990

'When I was in Paris, the night after the premiere, a box full of berets was delivered to my room at the Hotel George V. They were from a small village near Lourdes in the French Pyrenees, where the traditional French berets were made. After the release of *Bonnie and Clyde* (1967), demand had pushed production from 5,000 to 12,000 berets a week, and they wanted to thank me.'
Faye Dunaway, actress, 1995

'Cock your hat—angles are attitude.'
Frank Sinatra, inveterate hat-wearing actor and singer, 1915–98

Hourglass Silhouette

Mae West's out-and-out femininity struck a chord with Paris couturiers. Her spectactular belle epoque-style curves inspired Schiaparelli, as well as Marcel Rochas's creation of the *guêpière*, or waspie, a strapless combination of corset and girdle (1947) that was perfectly in tune with Dior's 'New Look' designs. While both designers created screen costumes for her, West's hourglass figure reputedly inspired the design of their scent bottles: both the flacon created by artist Léonor Fini for Schiaparelli's signature Shocking (1937) and the flacon for Rochas's Femme (1944–45).

'The Big Ben of hourglass figures.'
Truman Capote, American writer, on famously curvaceous actress Mae West, 1893–1980

'The Love Goddess . . . Aubrey Beardsley might have drawn the canary-white tendrils weaving over the hourglass figure as a landlocked mermaid.'
Cecil Beaton, photographer, designer, artist and aesthete, on Mae West's distinctive shape, 1986

'Cultivate your curves—they may be dangerous, but they won't be avoided.'
Mae West, Hollywood actress, playwright and screenwriter, 1959

'There's a broad with her future behind her.'
Constance Bennett, actress, 1904–65, on Marilyn Monroe

'Marilyn Monroe was another star who had the magic IT, which has nothing to do with clothes, except hers were cut to exact specifications at the bust and derrière.'
John Fairchild, publisher and author, 1965

'It' girl Clara Bow channels the confident, insouciant, vampish look that brought female sexual magnetism to the silver screen and placed it centre stage in the emancipated 1920s (1926).

Icons

'I never think of myself as an icon. What is in other people's minds is not in my mind. I just do my own thing.'
Audrey Hepburn, actress, 1929–93

'Marilyn Monroe was the sex goddess, Grace Kelly the ice queen, Audrey Hepburn the eternal gamine. Ms. Taylor was beauty incarnate.'
Mel Gussow, American journalist, 2011

Individuality

'Always be a first-rate version of yourself, instead of a second-rate version of someone else.'
Judy Garland, actress and singer, 1922–69

'We had individuality. We did as we pleased . . . we dressed the way we wanted. I used to whizz down Sunset Boulevard in my open Kissel, with several red Chow dogs to match my hair. Today, they're sensible and end up with better health. But we had more fun.'
Clara Bow, actress and original 'It' girl, who started a craze when she hennaed her hair, 1905–65

'Everything she did was individual—every gesture, every movement, every look, even the way she wore her clothes. Not the clothes, but the way she wore them . . . guaranteed you would look at her even if she hadn't been so beautiful.'
Charlotte Chandler, biographer, on Greta Garbo, 1985

I

'Fashion models could and did learn things from the young Garbo and the young Dietrich. These lessons could not then be found in other women, professional actresses or not. The fashion world has been using Garbo ever since she brought out her idiomatic style. For years now, rakishness, bold angularity, mock insolence, and the insinuation of an apparently uncontrollable pelvis have been the fashion model's stock-in-trade. Much more came from the Garbo of the 1920s and 1930s than people have supposed. The negligently slung hip, the cocked elbow and the space straddle were all Garbo's. I mean they were all hers as "originals," not as copies. There are no more Garbos; or Dietrichs, for that matter.'
Parker Tyler, film critic, 1963

'Everything Marilyn does is different from any other woman, strange and exciting, from the way she talks to the way she uses that magnificent torso.'
Clark Gable, actor, 1961

'A star must have individuality. It makes you a great star. A great star.'
George Cukor, director, 1899–1983

'Be yourself. The world worships the original.'
Ingrid Bergman, Swedish-born actress, 1915–82

Influence

'As the first thrilling bars of music herald the latest Greta Garbo, Joan Crawford or Norma Shearer production, you will notice, as the presentation unreels, the simple credit—"Gowns by Adrian." That is your cue to sit taut in your seat and strain all your faculties, for what you and you will next be wearing is about to be revealed!'
Helen Harrison, American journalist, 1932

'Hollywood is becoming the Paris of America. Consequently, when women go to the movies, they look to film divas as fashion role models.'
Adrian, Hollywood costume designer, 1933

'Your clothes come from Hollywood.'
Photoplay, *1929*

'The influence of the films can be traced in the clothes and appearance of the women and in the furnishing of their homes. Girls copy the fashions of their favourite film star.'
New Survey of London Life and Labour, *1930*

'Some fossils may still look to Paris for their fashions . . . but you and I know Paris isn't even a stand-in to Hollywood . . . that Paris may decree this and Paris may decree that, but when that Crawford girl pops up in puffed sleeves, then it's puffed sleeves for us before teatime.'
Wes Colman, journalist, on Joan Crawford's much-copied white Adrian dress in Letty Lynton *(1932)*

'We can often trace a prevailing style to some well-costumed drama, even though it is laid in bygone times. The actresses are mannequins in the women's eyes. It is the reason talking pictures are showing such an influence on current fashions. And why Hollywood, in turn, is becoming the arbiter in dress.'
Travis Banton, costume designer, 1894–1958

'Hollywood styles and fashions actually are far superior to those of Paris and other European capitals. We are going to prove to them that the clothes worn by Hollywood motion picture stars are months in advance of anything Paris can supply them.'
Hollywood Pavilion handbill accompanying a travelling show of film costumes at the Chicago World's Fair, 1933

'Hollywood, in fact, is now the Mecca not only of the majority of actresses, but of the majority of common or garden copyists.'
Herbert Farjeon, British theatre critic, lyricist, presenter and playwright, 1933

I

'The greatest fashion influence in America, stylists sadly lament, is the much-photographed, much-glamorized and much-imitated Movie Queen. What she wears is news, eagerly copied, by girls who want to look like Joan Crawford and Myrna Loy.'

'The Fashion Industry Bumps into Hollywood.' Click magazine, 1938

'The clothes we design up here are one year ahead of Paris and two years ahead of the manufacturers.'

Howard Greer, costume designer, 1949

'Via the high street or the sewing machine, the mantle of glamour passed from the aristocrat and courtesan to the shop, office or factory girl via the film star.'

Sally Alexander, British historian and academic, 1989

'With a receptive, even clamouring public ready to pounce on any new American talent, with the power of the movies here to promote dramatic ideas, the air of the American fashion world is teeming with excitement. But we are still pathetically poor in truly original and skilled designers. We are not so scholarly nor so lighthearted nor so courageous as the French. We have not learned to be gaga in the grand manner.'

Adrian, costume designer, 1934

'It is true that Hollywood introduced a new sense of fashion and beauty to the world, and, sad to say, also true that the designers of the clothes worn by the famous Hollywood film stars were never really given their full credit.'

Cecil Beaton, photographer, designer, artist and writer, 1981

'I always thought what the Hollywood designers had to do for the stars had a far greater influence on contemporary fashion than anything the French designers came up with.'

John Kobal, film historian, 1986

'I frankly don't remember any "fashion" before Adrian.'
Joan Crawford, actress, 1963

'In the last century there are only two people that really and truly had an influence on how men wanted to look. One of them was the Duke of Windsor. And the other was Mr. Gary Cooper.'
Bill Blass, American fashion designer, 1922–2002

'It' and the 'It' Girl

British novelist Elinor Glyn coined the term 'It' as a euphemism for sex appeal and sexual magnetism in the silent film era of the 1920s. The original 'It' girl, Clara Bow, starred in Glyn's 1927 film *It*, hence the popular moniker.

'"It" is that quality possessed by some which draws all others with its magnetic force . . . a purely virile quality belonging to a strong character, entirely unself-conscious, full of self-confidence, indifferent to the effect and uninfluenced by others. With "It" you win all men if you are a woman—and all women if you are a man.'
Elinor Glyn, British novelist and screenwriter, 1864–1943

'It isn't what I do, but how I do it. It isn't what I say, but how I say it, and how I look when I do it and say it.'
Mae West, actress, playwright, and screenwriter, 1893–1980

'It takes IT to make a star, just as it takes IT to make a fashion. I suppose the word is style, but . . . many of the girls in Hollywood certainly don't have style and yet they are supposed to be stars. Let's say the IT is spirit—spirit and fire in body and soul like Sophia Loren.'
John Fairchild, publisher and author, 1965

'He's got "It."'
Fred Astaire, actor, dancer, choreographer and singer, on seeing actor John Travolta's performance in Saturday Night Fever (1977), *1977*

I

James Dean's choice of jeans rather than a pristine suit gave Hollywood actors an alternative style code, and a generation of filmgoers their icon: young, cool and rebelliously casual (1955).

Jeans

Originally termed 'waist overalls' by Levi's, jeans were the practical uniform of countless western cowboys. However, jeans were given a completely new screen image when archetypal 1950s antiheroes Marlon Brando and James Dean branded them with rebel youth style, and Marilyn Monroe flaunted her curves in figure-hugging Levi's in *The Misfits* (1961).

'If I dressed for myself, I wouldn't bother at all. Clothes bore me. I'd wear jeans.'
Marlene Dietrich, German actress and singer, 1960

'I do not wear jeans.'
Sophia Loren, actress, rejecting Edith Head's initial casual costume sketches for Houseboat *(1958), 1958*

'Glamour is not all low-cut gowns and the slinky look. Blue jeans can still make you look attractive.'
Marilyn Monroe, actress, 1953

'She was poor, she wore blue jeans (an early popularizer of the now classic uniform) and a shirt. Her jeans, she would put on moist so that they would cling more easily to her contours.'
Eve Arnold, photographer, on the young Marilyn Monroe, 1989

'He was very conscious of his figure, which was so toned. I was an assistant to the designers on one of his early films, *The Sand Pebbles* (1966), and I still remember him trying on 30 pairs of Levi's before he found the pair he thought made his bottom look good enough to shoot.'
Theadora Van Runkle, costume designer, on actor Steve McQueen, 2010

'I'm like every other woman: a closet full of clothes, but nothing to wear. So I wear jeans.'
Cameron Diaz, actress, 1972–

Jewellery

Hollywood stars often wore their own jewellery in films. Many became jewellery aficionados, developing a serious jewellery obsession and amassing stones of considerable size and value—Joan Crawford's favourites were sapphires, which were known as 'Joan Blue,' while Paulette Goddard carried her diamonds around in a cigar box and swam in her diamond necklace.

'When my hair was in place, two women brought in my costume, a beautiful white day dress, and helped get it on over my hair. A few minutes later, Pinkerton detectives arrived with three velvet-lined jewel chests. Everything was real, and I was supposed to pick what I wanted to go with the dress. Mr. DeMille always had his actresses pick out the jewellery they wore in his films so that they would act as if they owned it. I chose a delicate necklace and earrings, and an assortment of rings and bracelets.'

Gloria Swanson, actress, 1980

'You must never put costume jewellery or imitation lace on Garbo. Not that it would be noticed on the screen, but it would do something to Garbo and her performance.'

Adrian, costume designer, 1903–59

'If a man sends me flowers, I always look to see if a diamond bracelet is hidden among the blossoms. If there isn't one, I don't see the point of flowers . . . I take nothing perishable!'

Hedy Lamarr, actress and jewellery collector, to fellow collector actress Zsa Zsa Gabor, 1992

'I never hated a man enough to give him his diamonds back.'

Zsa Zsa Gabor, actress, socialite and jewellery collector, 1957

'I have always felt a gift diamond shines better than one you buy for yourself.'

Mae West, actress, playwright and screenwriter, 1893–1980

"No gold-diggin' for me—I take diamonds.'
Mae West, actress, playwright and screenwriter, 1893–1980

'Without diamonds, honey, I'd feel undressed.'
Mae West, actress, playwright and screenwriter, 1959

'I designed 30 or 40 lbs of jewellery for Mae to wear as "Diamond Lil." I first found pictures of period jewellery to show her. "Fine, Honey," she said, "just make 'em *bigger*."'

Edith Head, costume designer, 1959

'My mother says I didn't open my eyes for eight days after I was born; but when I did, the first thing I saw was an engagement ring. I was hooked.'
Elizabeth Taylor, actress, and jewellery connoisseur, 1932–2011

'Big girls need big diamonds.'
Elizabeth Taylor, actress, famed for her king-sized jewels, 1932–2011

'[Audrey Hepburn] had the originality never to wear any jewellery, and this at the time of double rows of pearls, little earrings, lots of "little" everything . . . And then suddenly she would appear at a premiere wearing earrings that reached all the way down to her shoulders.'
Leslie Caron, French actress, 1993

Actress Mamie Van Doren exemplifies all the attributes of Hollywood's popular sweater girl pinups, who were often photographed in profile to further accentuate their feminine assets (1958).

Knitwear—Hollywood's Sweater Girls

A look first popularized in the late 1930s by a young Lana Turner in her first film, *They Won't Forget* (1937), this fashion transformed the conservative sweater into a glamorous and sexy essential as worn by Hollywood's eminent pinups. Figure-hugging sweaters, cardigans or twinsets flaunted the contours, which, by the 1950s, were increasingly emphasizing the bustline with the help of conical 'bullet' bras. As well as Lana Turner, the sweater girls of the 1940s and '50s (the latter decade being its heyday) included actresses as diverse as Jane Russell, Ann Sheridan, Kim Novak, Ava Gardner, Marilyn Monroe and Jayne Mansfield. A decade later, Faye Dunaway's retro-style knits, worn without underwear in *Bonnie and Clyde* (1967), created a fashion for an altogether different kind of sweater girl.

'Dramatic art, in her opinion, is knowing how to fill a sweater.'
Bette Davis, actress, on Jayne Mansfield, 1987

'Couldn't act her way out of her form-fitting cashmeres.'
Tennessee Williams, American writer and playwright, on Lana Turner, 1911–83

'Her dresses and sweaters, when she could afford them, she wore a size too small, to emphasize her curves.'
Eve Arnold, photographer, on the young Marilyn Monroe, 1989

'She created . . . a new style of young woman when all the rage was for aggressive bosoms and shapely hips.'
Lesley Caron, actress and dancer on Audrey Hepburn's impact, 1993

Hollywood icon Audrey Hepburn carries off Parisian haute couture with Hollywood pizzazz as the finest exponent of the little black dress in the seminal style film Breakfast at Tiffany's *(1961).*

Ladies

'Miss Monroe should be told that the public likes provocative feminine personalities, but it also likes to know that underneath it all, the actresses are ladies.'

Joan Crawford, actress, on Monroe's provocative dress and suggestive hip wiggle that drew wolf whistles at the Photoplay Awards, 1953

'Mostly we have manufactured ladies—with the exception of Ingrid, Grace, Deborah and Audrey.'

Cary Grant, actor, 1904–86, on his favourite leading ladies: the Misses Bergman, Kelly, Kerr and Hepburn

Legends

'Some clients, like Marlene Dietrich, know exactly what they want. They see big. They know how to feed the legend. But there are few like them.'

Ginette Spanier, directrice of the couture house of Balmain, 1959

'[Costume designer Travis] Banton and Dietrich built up almost a legend of an exotic, super, high-fashion look, which on another person would have looked ridiculous. She could get away with it. It was almost a signature—the feathers, the veils, the furs, the glitter, the glamour.'

Edith Head, costume designer, 1959

'There are people who know something is missing even in apparent perfection, and then there are those who realise it only after they are shown what it was. My mother was one of the former—most performers belong to the latter. It may be one of the subtle differences between legend and star.'

Maria Riva, daughter and biographer of Marlene Dietrich, 1992

Lingerie

'Such care was taken in those days. Even our petticoats were of the finest materials. Ribbons and lace, silk or chiffon, crystal pleats.'

Jane Powell, actress, 1929–

'Money was nothing at the time . . . this was the era BB (Before Budgets). A star's wardrobe for a picture included her handmade lingerie, whatever the lady wanted. Once, when [Howard] Greer was in Europe and [Travis] Banton on vacation, Garbo walked in. She was carrying a beautiful man's bathrobe she wished made over to fit her. This was my privilege.'

Edith Head, costume designer, 1959

'Jean Harlow was notorious for going braless. But this star was one who couldn't and wouldn't . . . Howard Hughes then decided it wouldn't be any harder to design a bra than it would be to design an airplane . . . and believe me, he could design planes, but a Mr. Playtex he wasn't.'

Jane Russell, buxom actress, on director and aeronautical designer Howard Hughes's attempt at a cantilevered support bra for her to wear on her first film, The Outlaw (1943), 1986

The Little Black Dress

Audrey Hepburn in couturier Hubert de Givenchy's designs immortalized the LBD onscreen. In *Sabrina* (1954), Givenchy invented the Sabrina neckline, a boat-neck style with narrow bows on each shoulder, then in *Breakfast at Tiffany's* (1961) another sleeveless shift, and, most famously of all, a long black column dress, accessorized with pearls and oversized sunglasses.

'I've always believed in the basic institution of the little black dress with a touch of white at the throat.'

Claudette Colbert, actress, who frequently appeared on the International Best-Dressed List, and was, for several years, voted Hollywood's Best-Dressed Woman, 1903–96

'That dress seemed marvellous from the first moment I thought of it. I think Rita made it sexy because of the casualness with which she wore it. There was something voluptuous about her ease.'

Jean Louis, 1907–97, costume designer, on his strapless black satin sheath dress for Rita Hayworth in Gilda *(1946), which was inspired by John Singer Sargent's notorious painting* Portrait of Madame X *(1884–5)*

'Audrey Hepburn and Givenchy were made for each other. His little black dress with shoestring straps in *Sabrina* (1954) must have been imprinted on many teenagers' minds forever.'

Barbara Hulanicki, designer, 1983

'She [Audrey Hepburn] raised the little black dress to an art form. She taught us how to wear it once and for all.'

Ellen Melinkoff, American writer, 1984

Luxury

'It was not long before my clothes bill assumed considerable proportions, and became quite a serious problem to the costing department of the studio! For gowns, negligées, accessories, hose and shoes, all were designed in the very latest and most exclusive fashions.'

Gloria Swanson, actress whose film contract obliged her to extend her onscreen image by wearing the latest fashions and opulent jewellery, which was bought at her own expense, when she appeared in public, 1932

'Imagine, and marvel at in retrospect, the dress worn by Marlene Dietrich in *Angel* in 1937, made of rubies, emeralds, topazes, and diamonds, a confection from the talents of Travis Banton.'

Cecil Beaton, photographer, designer, artist and writer, 1981

'Expensive things look expensive. There is always a connoisseur in the crowd.'

Marlene Dietrich, actress and singer, 1961

L

Marlene Dietrich's always-immaculate maquillage was an essential element of her perfectionist screen craft; cosmetics endorsed by Hollywood's stars became a lucrative business (1944).

Makeup

'Too bad most of us need it.'
Marlene Dietrich, actress and singer, 1961

'The relationship between the makeup man and the film star is that of accomplices in crime.'
Marlene Dietrich, actress and singer, 1901–92

'My face was always so made up it looked as though it had the decorators in.'
Shelley Winters, actress, 1975

'She uses no makeup save a dark line like a symbol on her eyelids . . . a symbol which only instinct created and yet which the world has copied.'
Cecil Beaton, photographer, designer, artist and writer, on Garbo's signature crescent-moon-shaped eyeliner, 1904–80

'The way you make up your lips, apply your rouge . . . ten to one, it came from Hollywood and was devised either by or for some famous star.'
British Vogue, 1937

'How far we have come since the little heart-shaped mouth of ladies in 1900! After the refined curve of the lips of Clara Bow in the 1920s, it was Joan Crawford's admirable large mouth and the natural, expressive mouth of Audrey Hepburn. Women's mouths today are spontaneous, joyous, sensual and free.'
Helena Rubinstein, founder of her eponymous cosmetics empire, 1965

'I never conceived an avid appetite for Joan Crawford as a screen heroine. I confess a preference for eyebrows which stay where they grew, lips which start where they begin and finish where they end.'
W. H. Mooring, British film critic, attributed

'Even when I'm home alone, I wear my lipstick. I feel naked without it.'
Bette Davis, actress, 1908–89

'I live by a man's code, designed to fit a man's world, yet at the same time I never forget that a woman's first job is to choose the right lipstick.'
Carole Lombard, actress, 1937

'The lipstick and the mascara were like clothes. They improved my looks as much as if I had put on a real gown.'
Marilyn Monroe, actress, 1926–62

'I have never felt good in makeup. I think you have to start using it early in life to feel natural when you have something unnatural on your face. I always feel people looking at my face will see where the makeup ends and I begin, especially in daylight. Even light makeup feels like a mask I'm wearing to hide behind. I do not want to hide. I wish to communicate. I wish to look like myself.'
Ingrid Bergman, actress famous for her natural beauty, 1915–82

'Decide what features you want to focus attention on . . . In my view, most girls look desirable with glistening lids and a moist mouth. A drop of oil on the lids will give the effect, and if you're handy with a lipstick brush, there's nothing like it for that luscious look.'
Marilyn Monroe, actress, 1953

'Marilyn has makeup tricks that nobody else has and nobody knows. She has certain ways of lining and shadowing her eyes that no other actress can do. She puts on a special lipstick, a secret blend of three different shades . . . then a gloss, a secret formula of Vaseline and wax.'
Whitey Snyder, Marilyn Monroe's makeup man, 1973

'I would rather lose a good earring than be caught without makeup.'
Lana Turner, actress, 1921–95

'I came out of the womb wearing makeup!'
Catherine Zeta-Jones, actress, 1969–

M

Men's Costume Design

In the early days of cinema, it was usual for actors to provide their own costumes. This was a custom that persisted for men: some, like Cary Grant, insisted on it. For *North by Northwest* (1959), Grant provided eight copies of the grey suit and twelve copies of the tie he wore. He also reserved a bolt of the suit cloth in case the suits were damaged during filming.

'Edith [Head] dressed the women but she didn't design my clothes. I planned and provided everything myself . . . I was the only one who approved my clothes. Hitch[cock] trusted me implicitly to select my own wardrobe. If he wanted me to wear something very specific he would tell me, but generally I wore simple, tasteful clothes—the same kind of clothes I wear off-screen.'
Cary Grant, actor, 1983

'I kept the same suit for six years and the same dialogue. They just changed the title of the picture and the leading lady.'
Robert Mitchum, actor, 1917–97

'The real moment of liberation for late-twentieth-century menswear is the film *American Gigolo* [1980].'
Richard Martin, costume historian, curator and writer, on the impact of Italian designer Armani's softly tailored wardrobe for Richard Gere's eponymous film character, which promoted Italian style and interest in clothing as a legitimate masculine pursuit, 1998

Minimalism
'Gary Cooper and I are the same. We're both minimalists. Less is more.'
Ernest Hemingway, writer, 1899–1961

'Without a huge clutter of worldly goods, and wearing old clothes, I feel—comfortable and free.'
Montgomery Clift, actor, heartthrob and major star who declined Hollywood's rampant consumerism, 1920–66

Mystique
'Suspense is like a woman. The more left to the imagination, the more excitement . . . The conventional big-bosomed blonde is not mysterious . . . the perfect "woman of mystery" is blonde, subtle and Nordic.'
Alfred Hitchcock, British director and connoisseur of blonde Hollywood actresses, 1957

'The only one who has ever been really mysterious.'
Joan Crawford, 1905–77, actress, on Greta Garbo

'Her mystery was as thick as London fog.'
Tallulah Bankhead, 1902–68, actress, on fellow actress, the elusive Garbo

'The old stars had a mystique and they clung to it even after everything else was gone. I mean, if they went out the back door to carry out the garbage, they dressed as though they were going to a charity ball. They dressed and lived and fed on that image of glamour. It may have been a make-believe world, but at least they worked at it.'
Gene Autry, American musician and actor, 1907–98

'Rita Hayworth belonged to the grand tradition of glamorous movie queens who were not only beautiful and talented but who also generated excitement by always retaining a certain aura of mystery and allusion. Ava Gardner has these qualities, too. In fact, Rita and Ava are truly the last members of that very distinctive breed: genuine glamour stars. Unfortunately, we just don't have superstars like them anymore. Today, actresses believe they must play down their beauty and be intellectual. But you have to be a Katharine Hepburn to get away with that. We now have "instant" superstars who are forgotten in a year or two. Once a woman forsakes her most cherished possessions, glamour and mystery, she simply can't hold anyone's attention for very long.'
George Cukor, director, 1977

'There's a mystery to them—I don't think any American personality of my generation had the glamour that was Dietrich and Garbo . . . we never had the mystery, the touch, these other women had. And never would.'
Ann Sheridan, actress, 1977

'It's an old rule that mystery, not diamonds, is a girl's best friend.'
William Travilla, costume designer, 1920–90

M

Rita Hayworth reputedly had the longest nails in Hollywood. A beautiful manicure was the key requisite for the Hollywood pinup along with styled hair, makeup and wardrobe (1946).

Nails

Uma Thurman's modish dark nails in *Pulp Fiction* (1994), courtesy of Chanel's 'Rough Noir' varnish (later called 'Vamp'), set a perennial fashion.

'Dark nail polish is vulgar.'
Marlene Dietrich, actress and singer, 1961

Necklines

'Necklines of a distinctive cut, and scarves, draped in all kinds of fantastic ways, serve to give a dress significance for me.'
Joan Crawford, actress, 1931

'She wore her dresses with the necklines so low she looked as though she had jumped into her dress and caught her foot on the shoulder straps.'
Jack Paar, actor, on his Love Nest (1951) costar Marilyn Monroe, 1982

Neutrals: The Colour Scheme Favoured by the Stars

'I belong to the traditional French school of wearing black as the most elegant . . . white suits me best; it's good for my eyes and my hair.'
Dolores del Río, actress, 1905–83

'Black and white are almost invariably my choice.'
Jean Harlow, actress on the colours that best set off her skin and hair, 1932

'Mae had written into her contract that she was the only one who would appear on screen dressed in black, white, or black-and-white. She always did that because whoever wears black-and-white in a Technicolor film immediately gets the audience's eye.'
Edith Head, costume designer, on Mae West's style strategy, 1959

'Whether in film or on stage, I have always preferred neutral colours to pure colours, and the experts with whom I have worked always agreed with me.'
Marlene Dietrich, actress and singer, 1989

'Don't let her kid you. She owns a 50-acre estate surrounded by a picket fence made of nothing but Oscars!' Walter Plunkett on fellow costume designer Edith Head, eight-time winner. (c.1955)

'One-note' Dressing

'Every costume should have one note. Concentration on that one note emphasizes it and makes it interesting. When you start to concentrate on more than one note, then you detract from the main idea and merely have a conglomeration. Sound one note truly, then it will have a definite value.'

Adrian, costume designer, 1933

Oscars

Some of Hollywood's finest costume designers were never honoured with an Oscar, since the award for best costume design was only inaugurated at the 21st Awards in 1948, after the designers Adrian, Travis Banton and Howard Greer had retired from film work (for example, in 1939 both Adrian and Walter Plunkett missed out, for *The Wizard of Oz* and *Gone with the Wind*, respectively). When it was finally introduced, the genre was divided: into black-and-white and colour film, with an award for best costume presented in each of the two categories, a practice that continued until 1967. Some costume Oscars were contentious, notably Edith Head's infamous 1954 award for Audrey Hepburn's costumes in *Sabrina*, the most elegant and stylish of which were selected by Audrey Hepburn in Paris from the couturier Hubert de Givenchy, who received no screen credit.

'It is said of Edith that the Oscar is written into her contract; she has more Oscars than anyone else in Hollywood.'

John Huston, director, screenwriter and actor, on prolific Oscar-winning costume designer Edith Head, 1980

'The Oscar ceremonies [are] the biggest fashion-watching event of this, and every, year.'

Bob Mackie, fashion and costume designer, 2000

'The Oscar night red carpet is a gridlock of haute couture.'

André Leon Talley, American fashion and style journalist, 2007

O

The platinum blonde, epitomized by its original incarnation, Jean Harlow, in Deco-style splendour, remains an enduring and powerful evocation of Hollywood style and glamour (1933).

Perfume

'Perfume reigned as a prize possession for the glamorous stars of the early days. Sam Kress, a druggist at the corner of Cahuenga Pass and Hollywood Boulevard, carried $250,000 worth of imported perfume in his store to satisfy the perfume craze. Pola Negri reportedly bought one of each of the scents . . . Some stars maintained a separate bedroom just to house their perfume collections.'
Veronica Lake, actress, 1969

'Carole Lombard wore her clothes like perfume . . . she could just sort of splash them on and forget about them.'
Travis Banton, costume designer, 1894–1958

'What do I wear in bed? Why, Chanel No. 5, of course.'
Marilyn Monroe, actress, in answer to a reporter, 1957

Platinum Blondes

Marilyn Monroe used the same hair colourist as Jean Harlow, the original platinum blonde, and described her own preferred hair colour as 'pillowcase white.'

'I've always hated my hair, not only because it limited me as an actress, but because it limited me as a person. It made me look hard and spectacular.'
Jean Harlow, actress and the original platinum blonde, 1911–37

'When she becomes platinum blonde, everything else changes, too. Suddenly there is a glow about her . . . everything about her becomes exaggerated.'
Eve Arnold, photographer, on the transformation of Marilyn Monroe, 1989

'What a fool I was to come to Hollywood, where they only understand platinum blondes.'
Bette Davis, American actress, 1908–89

Often symbolizing the Hollywood bad-boy outsider, the edgy style credentials of the quiff were established by James Dean, who made it the hairstyle with attitude and cool (1955).

Quality

'There is nothing better.'
Marlene Dietrich, actress and singer, 1961

'I'd rather have a few dresses of very fine material than a whole closetful of fussy, cheap-looking things . . . I find you don't tire of anything that is lovely in quality and line. It saves you money in the long run to get a good dress of which you're always proud and use it for two or three years.'
Jean Harlow, actress, who owned a Vionnet dress, 1932

'My father always said, "Buy the best of something. Inferior brands wear out."'
Cary Grant, actor, 1904–86

'[Audrey] rarely skimped on quality. If she wore a shirt it was a good shirt, a first-class shirt! Or a first-class hat! But simple.'
Audrey Wilder, wife of director Billy Wilder, on Audrey Hepburn, 1999

Queens

'I asked Bette Davis if she'd ever wanted to meet the Queen of England. "What for?" she snapped. "I am a queen."'
Natalie Wood, actress, on Bette Davis, who memorably played Queen Elizabeth I twice on film in The Private Lives of Elizabeth and Essex *(1939) and* The Virgin Queen *(1955), 1938–81*

'Susan Hayward was an ice queen—very like Grace Kelly that way.'
Robert Cummings, American actor, 1910–90

Quiffs

From James Dean and Elvis to Rock Hudson and Clint Eastwood, some of Hollywood's biggest stars have sported the quiff. Popular during the 1950s, the quiff—slicked back at the sides and rolled forward at the front—was a trademark of the young Tony Curtis, who liked showing off his luxuriant hair, and essential for John Travolta in *Grease* (1978).

Marlon Brando's leather jacket, jeans and T-shirt in The Wild One *bucked Hollywood's notion of masculine glamour and brought the moody maverick antihero centre stage (1953).*

Realism

'We moved from the era of camouflage to the era of honesty in clothes. Originally we used to dress an actress as a perfect package, ironing out her figure faults, squeezing her, padding her, making her look taller or smaller and dressing her according to the character. Now they all just want to look like themselves.'

Jean Louis, costume designer, 1979

Rebel Style

'[I] never expected it to have the impact it did. I was as surprised as anyone when T-shirts, jeans and leather jackets suddenly became symbols of rebellion. Sales of leather jackets soared.'

Marlon Brando, actor, on his 1953 film The Wild One, *1994*

Reclining Boards

The clinging bias-cut gowns worn by screen sirens Jean Harlow and Carole Lombard were prone to unsightly creasing and wrinkles when the actresses sat down to rest between takes. This meant the dress had to be removed for pressing; a time-consuming and costly interruption to filming. To get around this, costume designers enlisted the help of prop men and the reclining board, also known as a lean or slant board, was devised, supporting the actress in a near upright position, allowing her to rest while keeping costumes pristine; they are still in use today.

'There wasn't a costume in which she could lie, bend or sit . . . To afford her some small relaxation, we improvised a reclining board; it had armrests and was tilted at an angle, and there she'd lean between scenes in glittering splendour, the jewels winking from her hourglass gowns and dazzling from her throat, ears, wrists, and every finger.'

Edith Head, costume designer, on Mae West, 1983

Gary Cooper, whether debonair in a suit or the rugged star of Westerns, epitomized the all-around American male. Formal or informal, he provided a blueprint for popular masculine style (1943).

Savile Row

Savile Row tailors Fred and Louis Stanbury made Fred Astaire's white tie and tails for the film *Top Hat* (1935); Kilgour, French and Stanbury made Cary Grant's suits for Hitchcock's *North by Northwest* (1959); Anthony Sinclair of Conduit Street made Sean Connery's Bond suits for *Dr. No* (1962); Doug Hayward of Mount Street made Steve McQueen's suits for *The Thomas Crown Affair* (1968). Savile Row's Hollywood client list also included Marlene Dietrich and Katharine Hepburn.

'Bond [was] an ex-Eton type who mixed with the aristocracy, belonged to the most exclusive clubs, gambled in Monte Carlo and wore handmade silk shirts and Sea island cotton pyjamas. Once we had signed Sean Connery, we threw everything into grooming him for the part. We wanted to bring out all those features, which are the unmistakable James Bond hallmark. The casual but well-cut suits, the black, soft-leather moccasins . . . the silk kimonos—all these were carefully designed to work the Bond style into Sean's macho image.'
Albert 'Cubby' Broccoli, producer, 1998

'Steve never stopped feeling he was a delinquent . . . He worked for weeks until he mastered life in a suit. And in [*The*] *Thomas Crown* [*Affair*], the look was a good part of it. Steve was wearing $3,000 suits for the first time in his life. It took him a while to get the kind of fluid movement of someone who is not merely comfortable, but demands that sort of tailoring. But by the time production began, he had it down beautifully.'
Faye Dunaway, actress, on costar Steve McQueen and his Savile Row suits, 1995

Seduction

'I prefer a woman who does not display all her sex at once. I like women who are also ladies, who hold enough of themselves in reserve to keep a man intrigued. On the screen, for example, if an actress wants to convey a sexy quality, she ought to maintain a slightly mysterious air.'
Alfred Hitchcock, director, 1962

S

'She has exactly what I have been looking for. She is seductive without being sexy. Under an icy surface, she seems to burn with an inner fire that will do wonders on the screen.'
Alfred Hitchcock, director, on actress Grace Kelly, 1953

'In later years, whether she was in a ball gown, draped in furs or simply wrapped in her ubiquitous white terry-cloth robe, she had the knack of making the viewer think her completely nude beneath.'
Eve Arnold, photographer, on actress Marilyn Monroe, 1989

'I like Edith [Head]'s things 'cos they're allurin' without being vulgar. You know, to be allurin' you don't have to look indecent. I like gowns that have just a little insinuendo [sic] about 'em.'
Mae West, actress, playwright and screenwriter, on her choice of costume designer for her comeback film Myra Breckinridge *(1970), 1970*

Sex Symbols

'They never had sex symbols in films until I came. Or they called it somethin' else, 'cos nobody used the word "sex" til I used it in my play [*Sex* (1926)].'
Mae West, actress, playwright and screenwriter, 1969

'With Rita [Hayworth], you always had to design to show off her body— not her legs, but her body; I mean, you couldn't put her in a business suit. Not because the studio would have objected, but because that was her personality. Rita Hayworth was known for that, for being a beautiful woman, and people didn't want to see Rita Hayworth in a suit.'
Jean Louis, costume designer, 1986

'Dietrich made sex remote, Garbo made it mysterious, Crawford made it agonizing, but Monroe makes it amusing. Whenever a man thinks of Marilyn, he smiles at his own thoughts.'
Milton Shulman, Canadian critic and author, 1913–2004

S

'Marilyn Monroe was an authentic "sex symbol" because not only was she "sexy" by nature but she also liked being one—and she showed it . . . at a time when the censorship to which we all had to submit (cheerfully, I would say) no longer existed.'

Marlene Dietrich, actress and singer, 1989

'She [Marilyn Monroe] rocketed from obscurity to become our postwar sex symbol—the pinup girl of an age. Transfigured by the garish marvel of Technicolor and CinemaScope, she walks like an undulating basilisk, scorching everything in her path but the rosemary bushes.'

Cecil Beaton, photographer, designer, artist and writer, 1904–80

'Sex appeal is 50 per cent what you've got and 50 per cent what people think you've got.'

Sophia Loren, actress, 1934–

Shoes

From Dorothy's ruby slippers in *The Wizard of Oz* (1939) to Fred Astaire's two-tone correspondents, shoes have played a prominent role in Hollywood style. Italian shoemaker to the stars Salvatore Ferragamo invented the platform sole to help shorter actresses, and perfected its art for the petite Brazilian bombshell Carmen Miranda. While no femme fatale would be seen without her requisite heels, Audrey Hepburn's ballet flats persuaded women out of their stilettos, and remain a fashion favourite.

'Before a scene was shot, Garbo always asked her cameraman, "Is ze feets in?" Her concern was not to conceal her feet if the answer was yes, but to change out of the bedroom slippers she wore for comfort under even the most ornate costume.'

Frederick Sands and Sven Broman, Garbo biographers, 1979

'I don't know who invented the high heel, but all women owe him a lot.'

Marilyn Monroe, 1926–62, actress, devotee of Salvatore Ferragamo's shoes

'Shoes are more important than suits and dresses. Good shoes give elegance to your entire appearance. Buy one pair of good shoes instead of three pairs of bad quality.'

Marlene Dietrich, actress and singer, 1961

'I look at the feet first—and they usually tell me a great deal about the woman. Whether she pays attention to the little things.'

Joan Crawford, actress, 1931

'My father told me, "If you can't afford good shoes, don't buy any. If you can afford one pair, buy black, if two pairs, one black, one brown. But they must be good because even when they are old, they will always be seen to be good shoes."'

Cary Grant, actor, 1986

'There's no excuse for brown shoes past sundown . . . Or white shoes. Or anything grey, unless it's deep charcoal. Or blue, unless it's midnight blue. In fact, let's keep it simple: after dark, men should wear black.'

Frank Sinatra, actor and singer, 1915–98

'Shoes, like all adornment, should suggest, but never shriek, sex.'

Jayne Mansfield, actress and sex symbol, 1933–67

Shoulders

'Paris had padded shoulders before Adrian took them. He was very smart. They had just come out in Paris and weren't very important yet, but Adrian saw their possibilities. And he saw them particularly as, "What the hell do you do with a woman that has shoulders as broad as Joan Crawford? Take this new fashion of pads, make them even bigger and set a fashion with them."'

Walter Plunkett, on fellow costume designer Adrian, 1902–82

'Who would believe that my career would rest on Joan Crawford's shoulders!'

Adrian, costume designer, 1940

'In Hollywood, one special item of popularity has preceded me—that of the padded shoulders. I had started them to give women a slimmer waist. They proved the Mecca of the manufacturers. Joan Crawford had adopted them and moulded her silhouette on them for years to come. They became emphasized and monstrous. Adrian took them up with overwhelming enthusiasm.'
Elsa Schiaparelli, couturière, 1954

Simplicity
'Simplicity is Garbo's god—as it should be.'
Adrian, costume designer, 1930

'Adrian [Crawford's chosen Hollywood costume designer] taught me so much about drama. He dressed me in black for the dramatic [stills] picture. He said nothing must detract. Everything must be simple, simple, simple. Just your face must emerge. No one should say, "Oh, isn't that a lovely collar," or, "Oh, look at that necklace," "Aren't those earrings divine?"; he made me conscious of the importance of simplicity.'
Joan Crawford, actress, 1972

'Simplification is the best medicine for making a beautiful woman more beautiful.'
Edith Head, costume designer, 1959

'She looks marvellous in plain things . . . She must have simplicity, skilful design, and practically no ornamentation. Hers is elegance in the subtlest sense.'
Edith Head, costume designer, on her designs for Ingrid Bergman in Hitchcock's 1946 film Notorious, *1959*

'Cary was always beautifully dressed. But he wasn't a clotheshorse . . . His tastes were really very simple, elegant, but simple.'
Eva Marie Saint, actress, on her North by Northwest *costar, 2006*

'Permit me to suggest that you dress neatly and cleanly.'
Cary Grant, actor, 1963

'One of the most photographed movie stars in the world, she was, in a way, the first minimalist.'
Deirdre Fernand, writer, on Audrey Hepburn, 2007

'Simplicity was her trademark.'
Leslie Caron, actress and dancer, on Audrey Hepburn, 1993

Socks

'He wore enormously loud stockings [socks], which would draw your eyes to his feet, which were his thing . . . Remember how he walked? He always had his hand in his pocket, and the pants were a little short so you could see the stockings, so that you could see the feet.'
Sam Goldwyn, Jr., Hollywood producer, on Fred Astaire, 1988

Spectacle

'I want clothes that will make people gasp when they see them. I don't want to see any clothes anybody could possibly buy in a store!'
Cecil B. DeMille, director and producer, whose succinct formula for Hollywood success was 'Sex, Sets, Costumes,' 1881–1959

'10,000 yards of pleated chiffon . . . one million tiny blue sequins . . . 12 yards of curled white ostrich plumes . . . 55 dozen Chinese pheasant tails . . . these are a few of the items needed for the magnificent costumes designed by Adrian for *The Great Ziegfeld*.'
Souvenir programme for The Great Ziegfeld, *1936*

'Glamorous and romantic Hollywood design—the glorification of heroes and heroines. Beautiful women, handsome men. Everything was larger than life. The diamonds were bigger, the furs were thicker and more. The silks, velvets, satins and chiffons, and miles of ostrich feathers. Everything was an exaggeration of history, fiction, and the whole extraordinary world. The basis was perfect designing and incredible workmanship—the cut of décolletage, the embroidery, the mounting of a skirt, and miles and miles of bugle beads. The eye travelled, the mind travelled. In a maze of perfection and imagination.'

Diana Vreeland, former editor-in-chief of American Vogue, fashion consultant and curator, 1984

Star Status

'A real star never stops.'
Mae West, actress, playwright and screenwriter, 1893–1980

'I realized early on that Mayer [Louis B., Hollywood producer] was right; I was obliged to be glamorous. Fortunately, or unfortunately, I went a few steps beyond Mayer's expectations. If people wanted to see Joan Crawford the star, they were going to see Joan Crawford the star. They paid their money and they were going to get their money's worth. In my day, a star owed the public a continuation of the image that made her a star in the first place.'
Joan Crawford, actress, 1904–77

'She had a special outfit for answering the fan mail, and another for eating lunch alone at home, each one fully accessorized, and looking every inch the movie star.'
Joseph L. Mankiewicz, screenwriter, producer and director, on actress Joan Crawford, 1909–93

'I never go outside unless I look like Joan Crawford the movie star. If you want the girl next door, go next door.'
Joan Crawford, actress, 1904–77

'To be a star is to own the world and all the people in it. After a taste of stardom, everything else is poverty.'
Hedy Lamarr, actress, 1914–2000

S

'That was a different era, when stars were pampered and petted by the studios so that they would feel like great exotic creatures. And I was lucky enough to be on the tail end of it.'
Faye Dunaway, actress, 1995

'[For] these people, who worked each day in make-believe . . . maintaining mystery and protecting it was extremely important. Movie stars, and all that label represented, did not mingle with the masses. Today, this would be condemned as snobbism, but not then. The public would have felt cheated had these "celestial beings" shown the slightest inclination towards normalcy. They expected, and got, their idols always beautiful, always glamorous, always handsome, unreal, perfect, divine.'

Maria Riva, daughter and biographer of Marlene Dietrich, 1992

'The majority of female stars today deliberately do not project an image. Their point of view is that the star idea is old-fashioned. Faye Dunaway may be one of the only exceptions who realizes that glamour and having a consistent look mean something to the public. The new stars couldn't care less. Now they're more into projecting themselves as artists . . . They talk about the movie they want to direct, not the movie they want to star in. It's a different world!'

Edith Head, costume designer, 1983

Starlets

'Some young Hollywood starlets remind me of my grandmother's old farmhouse—all painted up nice on the front side, a big swing on the backside, and nothing whatsoever in the attic.'

Bette Davis, actress, 1908–89

Style

'A star knows how to place herself, where to sit, when to talk, how to move, how to have a style all her own. Garbo is still supreme.'

John Fairchild, publisher and author, 1965

'Style, a semi-mental, semi-physical quality, is more superficial than other characteristics [beauty, personality, charm, temperament]. It depends not merely upon clothes, but upon an innate knowledge of how to walk, how to stand, how to conduct oneself generally. The *ability* to *wear* clothes is no small asset.'

Marshall Neilan, American actor, screenwriter, director and producer, 1922

S

'She [Dietrich] was wearing a black Balenciaga dress embroidered at the left breast with the scarlet bar of the Legion d'Honneur. But . . . the black dress was littler and subtler than volumes of *Vogue* could imply, and her single decoration was somehow more worldly and wicked than all the jewellery in Paris, London and New York put together.'
Cynthia Kee, journalist, 1960

'Errol [Flynn] was probably the most beautiful man I ever saw, his perfect body equally at home in a swimsuit or astride a horse . . . when he walked into a room, it was as if a light had been turned on. Errol always had style, honey. Real style.'
Ava Gardner, actress, 1922–90

'Very few people can wear a [historical] costume like he could . . . he did it with such style and such grace.'
Vincent Sherman, director, on Errol Flynn, 1986

'Edith, we are now in France. People dress here. It's the place where style is created—so do it.'
Alfred Hitchcock, director, instructs Edith Head on her costume designs for To Catch a Thief *(1955), set on the fashionable French Riviera, 1955*

'He was an exceedingly rare example of one whose standards of civility and style followed him, seamlessly, whenever he stepped off-set.'
GQ on actor Gregory Peck, 2010

'She [Audrey Hepburn] brought something new to the screen. Her European upbringing. She had a Dutch mother and an English father. You have to remember, she experienced the war under the Nazis, so she wasn't a typical American. So she brought her experiences to her sense of style, and that difference was appealing.'
Gregory Peck, actor and Audrey Hepburn's costar in Roman Holiday *(1953), 1999*

S

'In film after film, Audrey wore clothes with such talent and flair that she created a style, which in turn had a major impact on fashion. Her chic, her youth, her bearing, and her silhouette grew ever more celebrated, enveloping me in a kind of aura or radiance that I could never have hoped for. The Hepburn style had been born, and it lives today.'

Hubert de Givenchy, Parisian couturier, friend of Audrey Hepburn's, 1998

'Marilyn Monroe was not interested in costumes. She was not a clotheshorse. You could put anything on her you wanted. If it showed something, then she accepted it . . . as long as it showed a little something.'

Billy Wilder, director and screenwriter, 1999

'You can acquire chic and elegance, but style itself is a rare thing. The only people I can think of who have it [in Hollywood] are Audrey Hepburn and Betty [Lauren] Bacall.'

Irene Sharaff, costume designer, 1967

'She was short . . . she was overloaded with hair and bosom, a dreadnought of glamour rather than an elegant swan.'

Cathy Horyn, journalist, on Elizabeth Taylor, 2011

'Gene Kelly was like a Jeep, and Fred Astaire was a Rolls-Royce.'

Tommy Steele, British singer, dancer and actor, 1936–

'I was the Marlon Brando of dancers and Fred was the Cary Grant. My approach was completely different . . . the sort of wardrobe I wore—blue jeans, sweatshirt, sneakers—Fred wouldn't have been caught dead in. Fred always looked immaculate in rehearsals; I was always in an old shirt.'

Gene Kelly, actor, dancer, singer and choreographer, 1988

'He had style. His clothes were always very casual, and terribly, extremely, elegant, he had such taste.'

Audrey Hepburn, actress, on Fred Astaire, 1988

'Astaire's ability to appear elegant, dressy, relaxed, and somewhat sporty, all at the same time . . . construct[ed] a new model for male nonchalance, and everyone from Giorgio Armani and Ralph Lauren to the latest Italian designers has learned more than a thing or two from him.'
G. Bruce Boyer, writer on fashion and style, 2004

'When I first started to be able to afford to dress properly, I went to [fashion designer, Roy] Halston, and he said, "Well, what do you want to look like?" And I said, "During the day I want to look like Fred Astaire, and at night I want to look like a movie star."'
Liza Minnelli, actress and singer, 1988

'Movie stars today are not projecting their own style . . . they're wearing runway [catwalk] style. Instead of the stars influencing the fashion designers, it's the designers influencing them.'
Amy Spindler, journalist, 1998

'I don't think that there are any real style icons in Hollywood—not like the Monroe days. Actresses are so overdone by their stylists and the media, it is difficult to actually see their own personal style.'
Alexander McQueen, British fashion designer, 2000

The Suit

'It's sort of a mystery. Other men wear suits, but with other men, there's the man and then there's the suit on him. That didn't happen to Cary Grant. Style was like skin to him.'
Eva Marie Saint, actress and Grant's costar in North by Northwest (1959), 1924–

'*North By Northwest* isn't a film about what happens to Cary Grant, it's about what happens to his suit.'
Todd McEwen, novelist and writer, 2006

'Cary Grant's tailored grey, vent-less, three-button suit in the 1959 Alfred Hitchcock thriller *North By Northwest* is arguably the most legendary in the history of American cinema.'

Adam Rapaport, style editor, GQ magazine, 2006

'My father used to say, "Let them see you and not the suit. That should be secondary."'

Cary Grant, actor, 1904–86

'[Cary Grant] seemed just as comfortable in a suit and tie as someone else would be in a pair of sweats. I can't even imagine him owning a pair of sweats or a T-shirt.'

Eva Marie Saint, actress, 1924–

'You want to know how I feel about clothes? I just take a new suit and roll it into a ball and throw it against the wall, and that way it becomes an old suit overnight. That's how I feel about clothes . . . The way to wear clothes is to tell them who's boss in the beginning. Then they fit you.'
Fred Astaire, actor, dancer, choreographer and singer, on his habit of 'breaking in' new clothes, 1988

'In order to ensure the wrinkle-free fit of his custom-made suits, Sinatra avoided sitting down; if this couldn't be avoided, he wouldn't cross his legs . . . day or night, his shirt cuffs had to extend one inch from his jacket sleeves, and his trouser legs were a hair's breadth above his polished shoes. He completed the look with classic monochrome ties, always silk, precisely folded breast-pocket handkerchiefs, gold cufflinks and a fedora hat.'
Simone Werle, writer, on Frank Sinatra's sartorial rules, 2010

'He was just such a sharp individual . . . His style was about simplicity, and keeping things clean-cut. And he could pull off an amazing slim suit.'
GQ acclaim the suit style of actor Sidney Poitier, 2010

'His style was sharp . . . clean as Ajax.'
Bernard Lansky, purveyor of suits to Elvis Presley, 2002

Sunglasses
'With my sunglasses on, I'm Jack Nicholson. Without them, I'm fat and 60.'
Jack Nicholson, actor, 1997

Swimwear
With the lavish spectacle of the aqua-musical in the '30s, '40s and early '50s, Hollywood put the spotlight on swimwear, transforming the swimsuit from an essentially mundane piece of sportswear into a fashionable must-have. Hollywood swimming 'costumes' were promoted by pinup images, from Betty Grable, to the swimming and diving sensation Esther Williams—dubbed the 'Million Dollar Mermaid' after her 1952 film.

Fred Astaire cuts a dash in signature top hat and tails: 'with his quick physical wit, his incredible agility, he belongs to a fantasy world as free as Mickey [Mouse]'s from the law of gravity' (1935).

Tailoring

'If you want the most elegant female in the world, you put Dietrich in a tailored suit—the plainer the suit, the more elegant she is.'
Edith Head, costume designer, 1959

'Carole [Lombard] loved tailored clothes; she hated dresses that looked, she said, "like a cross between French pastry and a lampshade."'
Edith Head, costume designer, 1959

'Sam Goldwyn refused to carry anything in his pockets because he was so determined to show off the cut of his suit—even a single coin, he felt, might ruin the immaculate look.'
Philip French, film critic and author, 1969

'[Cary Grant] and his slim-line clothes developed such an ideal one-to-one love affair that people could grin appreciatively in the sheer pleasure of observing the union.'
Pauline Kael, American film critic, 1975

'The Cary Grant clothes, all worsted, broadcloths and silks, all rich and underplayed, like a viola ensemble.'
Tom Wolfe, American writer, 1965

'At Barneys [a New York luxury department store] and elsewhere in the clothing industry, Cary Grant and Fred Astaire are still yardsticks for tailored elegance, used by every window dresser when coordinating men's merchandise for display.'
Simon Doonan, creative ambassador-at-large, newspaper columnist and writer, 1998

Tanning

Cary Grant's all-year-round tan was a way to avoid wearing heavy screen makeup, which he loathed, and was modelled on the example of an earlier style-setting tan fan, Douglas Fairbanks, Sr., whom the young Grant greatly admired and met on his 1920 journey to New York on the RMS *Olympic* as part of the Pender acrobatic troupe.

Taste
'Knowing what you cannot do is more important than knowing what you can do. In fact, that's good taste.'
Lucille Ball, actress, comedienne and television star, 1911–89

Top Hat and Tails
'At the risk of disillusionment, I must admit that I don't like top hats, white ties and tails.'
Fred Astaire, actor, dancer, choreographer and singer, 1960

'I learned from him a little lesson that I always remember: when you see people in tails and the white [waistcoat] hangs down under the black jacket, you know they have really ruined the line of the whole outfit. Fred Astaire always wore his waistcoat very high, and the jacket would just cover the white, which of course made his legs go on forever . . . if you watch films from the thirties, tails were always like that, but later on tails became an obsolete thing, and people didn't know how to wear them properly.'
Bob Mackie, fashion and costume designer, 1988

'I was strong as an ox. But if I put on a white tails and tux like Astaire, I still looked like a truck driver . . . I looked better in a sweatshirt and loafers anyway. It wasn't elegant, but it was me.'
Gene Kelly, actor, dancer, singer and choreographer, 1912–96

Trademarks
'You've got to have a gimmick!'
Veronica Lake, actress famous for her peek-a-boo hairstyle, on the need to stand out in Hollywood, 1969

'What Grace has is an elegance all her own; the white gloves are a trademark, so is the smooth hair.'
Edith Head, costume designer, 1959

'In the early days of the motion picture industry, even as late as the 1950s, stars still had trademarks: Jean Harlow with her white satin dresses; Dietrich with her tailored slacks; Garbo with her slouch hats and the trench coats; and Marilyn Monroe with her slightly tousled hair and tight clothes. But as we moved into the 1960s, the female stars didn't really care what they wore on the set or off. It was as if individualism had been thrown out the window in the name of realism.'
Edith Head, costume designer, 1983

The Trench Coat

An essentially British garment, made by firms like Burberry and Aquascutum, and originally popularized by British military officers in the First World War. The trench coat is a defining feature of Hollywood film noir characters; immortalized onscreen by Humphrey Bogart, it was worn by everyone from gangsters and their molls, hoodlums and spies to detectives and private eyes.

'Usually he wore the trench coat unbuttoned, just tied with the belt, and a slouch hat, rarely tilted.'
Peter Bogdanovich, director and writer, on Humphrey Bogart's signature film noir look, 2004

'Almost every man looks more so in a belted trench coat.'
Sydney J. Harris, journalist, 1917–86

'I only wear the trench coat because I desperately want to look like Robert Mitchum.'

Robert Stack, actor, 1919–2003

'From Robert Mitchum to *The Matrix* (1999) and beyond, the trench's role in cinema is undeniable. Some of the most dramatic and romantic moments in film are inextricably bound with one and, moreover, the trench is a signature of film's foremost style icons.'

Nick Foulkes, journalist and writer, 2007

Trousers

'First, I uncovered my legs, and people were excited over that. Now I cover my legs and that excites them, too.'

Marlene Dietrich, actress and singer, 1933

'From that second on, women all over the world leapt into trousers . . . fat women, thin women, tall women, short women, young and old women the whole world over thought that by jumping into trousers they could look like Marlene. Every photo that appeared of her sold thousands of pairs of trousers to more women and swamped the shops with their sales. The war, not many years later, spread the habit further as women war workers everywhere took to slacks.'

Mercedes de Acosta, writer and socialite, 1960

'The French press were critical of Dietrich's insistence on wearing male attire. They editorialized that "ladies" do not flout convention. The French fashion industry, then exclusively for women, was an important part of the country's economy, so one can understand their panic at the prospect of the female population casting off their restrictive frills for the comfort of a pair of trousers. Although Hermès was showing trousers for women as early as 1930 . . . the story mushroomed into an international mini-scandal. This did not stop Dietrich from wearing her pinstriped suits as she walked up the Champs Elysées.'

Maria Riva, daughter and biographer of Marlene Dietrich, 1992

'Slacks are all right for knockin' around the house, but not for knockin' around with men.'
Mae West, Hollywood actress, playwright and screenwriter, 1893–1980

'I love clothes. I always have loved to dress, and I'm uncomfortable unless I feel well-dressed . . . Slacks? Never! I abominate them. I like feminine things.'
Dolores del Río, actress and noted Hollywood beauty, 1905–83

'How can I do a picture with a woman who has dirt under her fingernails and always wears pants?'
Spencer Tracy, Hollywood actor, on his costar and partner, Katharine Hepburn, quoted by Patty Fox, 1999

'I like to move fast, and wearing high heels was tough, and low heels with a skirt is unattractive. So pants took over.'
Katharine Hepburn, actress, on her reasons for wearing trousers, 1907–2003

'I just had good timing. The times fit me. Pants came in, low heels came in.'
Katharine Hepburn, actress, 1907–2003

'In 1930, she wore pants and suits considered scandalous; today they are sensational.'
Calvin Klein, American fashion designer, honours Katharine Hepburn in the citation for her Lifetime Achievement Award on behalf of the Council of Fashion Designers of America, 1986

T

Marlon Brando established underwear as outerwear as the ubiquitous T-shirt became a youth-oriented style statement as Hollywood picked up on, then influenced, popular style culture (1951).

Understatement

'American "cool" started with Astaire's fine art of understatement.'
G Bruce Boyer, writer on style, 2004

'Everybody used him as an example of the well-dressed man, and he put that down by saying he didn't focus on being well dressed, he merely dressed moderately.'
Rick Ingersoll, on Cary Grant, 1991

'She never dressed to excite attention; she never dressed as an actress; she dressed like Grace Kelly.'
Edith Head, costume designer, 1959

'I created the "Grace Kelly look" for her; I put her in subdued, elegant dresses that set off her patrician good looks. I told her that her beauty should be set off like a great diamond in very simple settings. The focus was always to be on her.'
Oleg Cassini, fashion and costume designer, 1989

'She [Audrey Hepburn] always underdressed instead of overdressed. Nobody in the world looked better in plain white pants and a white blouse. Whatever she put on became perfectly elegant. Without a stick of jewellery, she looked like a queen.'
Eva Gabor, actress and socialite, 1993

'They are clothes without ornament, with everything stripped away. You can wear Hubert [de Givenchy]'s clothes until they are worn out and still look elegant.'
Audrey Hepburn, actress, on her favourite designer, 1929–93

Underwear

'I don't like to feel wrinkles.'
Marilyn Monroe, actress, on why she didn't wear underwear, 1926–62

'Fancy underwear has no attraction for me. All these be-laced foundation garments seem to me to prevent a dress from having the smooth flowing line that it should. I wear silk shorts—which I buy by the dozens in the children's department—and I walk straight by the crêpe de Chine fussies!'
Joan Crawford, actress, 1931

'Underwear makes me uncomfortable.'
Jean Harlow, actress famed for not wearing anything under her clinging dresses, 1911–37

'All those lines and ridges in undergarments are unnatural and they distort a girl, so I never wear them.'
Marilyn Monroe, actress, 1926–62

Just as Clark Gable caused a fashion frisson by dispensing with an undershirt in the 1934 film *It Happened One Night* (sales of undershirts plummeted dramatically), in *A Streetcar Named Desire* (1951), Marlon Brando caused a bigger stir by moodily sporting the (sweat-stained) undershirt as a garment, with sex appeal, in its own right; the T-shirt, an enduring emblem of youth and street style, has never looked back. The impact of both films proved that men as well as women were susceptible to Hollywood style.

'I came out here with one suit and everybody said I looked like a bum. Twenty years later Marlon Brando came out with only a sweatshirt and the town drooled over him. That shows how much Hollywood has progressed.'
Humphrey Bogart, actor, 1899–1957

'Fred Astaire wore a full set of long underwear under all his costumes when he danced. It absorbed the perspiration. And, of course, it never made any extra bulk, because there wasn't any there. They were cotton long johns with a top, all in one piece.'
Bob Mackie, costume designer, reveals another side of Astaire's screen style, 1988

Unexpected

'Garbo wears the unexpected. It is out of the unexpected that style is born, and the influence comes.'

Adrian, costume designer, 1932

USP

'Mae West . . . created her own silhouette, colour scheme and subaqueous flow of movement . . . It is a creation on a grand scale . . . She remains a phenomenon.'

Cecil Beaton, photographer, designer, artist and writer, 1986

'Nobody dressed Elvis Presley better than Elvis Presley . . . In that sense he was like a male version of Mae West: he knew the Elvis look.'

Edith Head, costume designer, 1983

'Everyone imitated my fuller mouth, darker eyebrows. But I wouldn't copy anybody. If I can't be me, I don't want to be anybody. I was born that way!'

Joan Crawford, actress, 1972

'Monroe's incandescence has been explained as a result of her alabaster skin and platinum hair, but her masseur Ralph Roberts said it was more than that. "The skin layer right under the surface is moist and deep, like no other woman's. In the dark, her skin could light up a room."'

Truman Capote, writer, 1955

'There's a whole new crop of important young actresses. The difference between them and the actresses of the past is that none of these girls have what you would call a trademark. In other words, Mae West is Mae West. She established something which was a definite person. The same for Joan Crawford and all of the really great stars. The thing today is not to be eccentric and unusual. Everybody is still to a degree an individual, but they do their own thing as a part of the look of now. I'm thinking of the girls like Jane Fonda, Katharine Ross, Jacqueline Bisset, Ali McGraw.'

Edith Head, costume designer, 1974

U

Louise Brooks still looks thoroughly modern today; her precise jazz age bobbed hair has continued to define women and influence film, from Cabaret *(1972) to* Chicago *(2002). (c. 1928).*

Vamp (an Abbreviation of "Vampire")

The seductress who led men astray originally had darkly gothic looks with dark hair, daringly revealing costumes and black-rimmed eyes, thanks to Helena Rubinstein's innovation of mascara. The original vamp Theda Bara was perhaps cinema's earliest sex goddess in the first of several temptress roles in *A Fool There Was* (1915). After the exotic Pola Negri took up Bara's siren mantle, followed by the stylish Louise Brooks and redhead Clara Bow, the vamp then metamorphosed into the femme fatale as exemplified by Marlene Dietrich, Greta Garbo and Rita Hayworth.

'The reason good women like me and flock to my pictures is that there is a little bit of vampire instinct in every woman.'
Theda Bara, actress and the original vamp, 1885–1955

'The completely charming *vamp de luxe* of the screen.'
Hollywood description of actress Jean Harlow, who changed the early dark-haired image of the vamp with her white-blonde hair and white slinky gowns, 1932

Vanity

'A vain woman is continually taking out a compact to repair her makeup. A glamorous woman knows she doesn't need to.'
Clark Gable, actor, who was married to Carole Lombard, one of Hollywood's most glamorous women, 1901–60

'Gina [Lollobrigida] has a star's compulsive vanity. She has 300 dresses and 70 pairs of shoes, keeps 15 handsome, leather-bound scrapbooks filled with newspaper clippings about Gina; one scrapbook is devoted entirely to observations about her bosom.'
Time *magazine, 1954*

'What's wonderful is he's got no vanity. I suppose when you're that good looking, you don't have to worry about vanity.'
Terry Gilliam, director, on actor and style icon Johnny Depp, 2000

'Life typecasts us. Look at me. Do you think I would have chosen to look like this? I would have preferred to have played a leading man in life. I would have been Cary Grant.'
Alfred Hitchcock, director, 1985

'In a woman celebrated for her beauty as she was, it surprised me to find hardly a trace of vanity. She would change her clothes several times a day . . . but that was not vanity. She just enjoyed it.'
John David Morley, British writer, on actress Elizabeth Taylor, 1984

'Vanity is my favourite sin.'
Al Pacino, American actor, 1940–

Vaselinos
The term for men imitating Rudolph Valentino's sleek, slicked-back hair, due to the copious use of Vaseline to achieve the effect; sharp dressers like actor George Raft epitomized the look in the 1930s and '40s. The effect of Valentino's hair was likened to shiny black patent leather.

Vintage
'The first poster girl for thrift-shop chic.'
Pamela Klaffke, writer, on Diane Keaton in Annie Hall *(1977), 2003*

Vital Statistics
'Nobody understands my body as well as my Hollywood designer.'
Barbara Stanwyck, Hollywood actress, 1907–90

'Bette [Davis] told me that when an actress signed a long-term contract with a Hollywood studio in the old days, she was dressed in something revealing, like a swimming costume, and was then asked to stand on a revolving podium in the middle of the sound stage. The platform was lit ruthlessly with floodlights, and as it revolved, all of the department heads, the cameramen, the makeup artists, the hairdressers, the designers, would sit around it with

clipboards, making notes about every single defect—the bust, the hips, the nose. She said it was the most appalling, humiliating experience, but it paid off in the end because one knew that one would never be seen at a disadvantage on the screen. Everyone at the studio was invested in preventing the public from seeing any type of physical imperfection one might have.'

Anthony Powell, British costume designer, 2003

'That's what most women haven't learned. They should study themselves critically in the mirror from all angles. There would be fewer mistakes. I had the advantage of studying films and stills [of myself].'
Claudette Colbert, actress, 1903–96

'You have to be absolutely frank with yourself. Face your handicaps, don't try to hide them. Instead, develop something else.'
Audrey Hepburn, actress, 1929–1993

'She handles her body like a Stradivarius used to handle his violins. And no matter what kind of finish it happens to be wearing at the time, it is still a masterpiece.'
John Barrymore, actor, on Marlene Dietrich, attributed

Volcanic appeal
'Elizabeth Taylor is volcanic . . . all gusto and fire. She lived life to its fullest. There hasn't been anyone quite like her.'
Camille Paglia, writer and academic, 1947–

'A snow-topped volcano.'
Alfred Hitchcock's description of actress Grace Kelly, attributed

Voluptuousness
'She had a quality of languor, a stillness filled with voluptuousness.'
Vinicius de Moraes, poet, on actress, Rita Hayworth, 1947

'She's the mostest.'
Frank Sinatra, actor and singer, on Sophia Loren, 1957

'I often dressed Sophia Loren. I can still see her looking somewhat chubby after a holiday feast, and then slipping into her fabulous handmade Italian corset to become the tiny-waisted voluptuous siren in *Houseboat* (1958).'
Edith Head, costume designer, 1983

V

'Everything you see I owe to spaghetti.'
Sophia Loren, actress, 1934–

Vulgarity

'Oh, I'm never dirty, dear, I'm interestin' without being vulgar. I have taste. I kid sex. I was born with sophistication and sex appeal but I'm never vulgar. Maybe it's breedin'.'
Mae West, actress, playwright and screenwriter, 1970

'New York and Paris disdainfully looked down their noses at the dresses we designed in Hollywood. Well, maybe they were vulgar, but they did have imagination. If they were gaudy, they but reflected the absence of subtlety which characterized all early motion pictures. Overemphasis . . . was essential. If a lady in real life wore a train one yard long, her prototype in reel life wore it three yards long. If a duchess at the Court of St James perched three feathers in her pompadour, the cinematic duchess perched six, just to be on the safe side. Into this carnivalesque atmosphere I was plummeted. There I wallowed in rhinestones and feathers and furs and loved every minute of it.'
Howard Greer, costume designer and author, 1949

'Vulgarity begins when imagination succumbs to the explicit.'
Doris Day, actress and singer, 1922–

'Nothing risqué, nothing gained!'
Jayne Mansfield, actress, 1933–67

'I know I'm vulgar, but would you have me any other way?'
Elizabeth Taylor, actress, 1932–2011

From Jean Harlow's satin gowns to John Travolta's disco suit, white holds a special place in Hollywood style, often relaying sex appeal, as in Monroe's dress in The Seven Year Itch *(1955).*

The Art of the Walk

'Like Chaplin, she built her film character around her walk.'
Eve Arnold, photographer, on Marilyn Monroe's unique hip sashay, 1989

'Marilyn does two things beautifully—she walks and she stands.'
Billy Wilder, director and screenwriter, 1999

'I'm more of a man's woman. I sashay up to a man. I walk up to a woman.'
Elizabeth Taylor, actress, 1932–2011

War-work Wardrobe

When Marlene Dietrich departed for 'Destination Unknown' [entertaining Allied troops during World War II], according to *Vogue* her 55-pound baggage allowance comprised: two long sequinned gowns, heavily encrusted with beads so no crease would show, a strapless brocade dress, transparent vinylite slippers, grey flannel men's trousers, a silk-lined cashmere sweater by Mainbocher, tropical uniforms and lingerie. She also carried a three-month supply of cosmetics labelled in huge nail-polish letters (for dressing by torchlight), and specially made soap for her hair which would lather in practically no water.

Weight

'Your body is the result of what you eat, as well as what you don't eat.'
Gloria Swanson, actress, 1899–1983

'I never worry about diets. The only carrots that interest me are the number of carats in a diamond.'
Mae West, actress, playwright and screenwriter, 1893–1980

'I was up to 142 lbs. . . . and I couldn't get the weight off in time so I figured I'd get Victor McLaglen. He's not only tall but wide . . . he'd make me look thin.'
Mae West, actress, playwright and screenwriter who cast all of her leading men, 1893–1980

'I'm not overweight. I'm just nine inches too short.'
Shelley Winters, actress, 1920–2006

Westerns

'I figured a good Western hat and a good pair of boots, and what's in-between is unimportant, which is the way most fellas were in those days.'
John Wayne, actor, 1907–79

'Since the hat is rarely taken off, not even in a house, it's very important. If you don't get the hat right, you may as well not get on a horse.'
Anthony Mann, director, on the Western's most important item of clothing, 1950

'I kept my own Western costume for most of my films. The hat, in particular. I wore it in every Western until one very sad day it completely disintegrated.'
James Stewart, actor, 1966

'Dad was a true Westerner.'
Maria Cooper Janis, daughter of actor Gary Cooper, 2011

'My father wore white tie and tails as easily as he wore jeans and cowboy boots.'
Maria Cooper Janis, daughter of actor Gary Cooper, 2011

White

'Heroes [and heroines] wear white.'
Anon, quoted by Patrizia von Brandenstein, costume designer responsible for John Travolta's off-the-peg white polyester three-piece suit in Saturday Night Fever (1977)

'She was happiest in white, but would switch to beige or black for contrast. It was rare for her to wear colour.'
Eve Arnold, photographer, on Marilyn Monroe, 1989

The explosive impact of West Side Story *(1961) propelled American youth culture and its urban street style centre stage. Its main hallmarks—jeans, chinos, sneakers—remain cool and current.*

X-Certificate

'She's not Madame X. She's Brand X; she's not an actress, she's a commodity.'
Pauline Kael, film critic, on actress and sex symbol Lana Turner in the 1966 film Madame X, *1966*

'The idea of suggesting undress has always been more seductive than stark nakedness. The naughtiest lady in pictures, or anyplace else, is more sex-alluring when slightly covered and *suggesting* her possibilities than enticing *sans raiment*.'
Robert Kalloch, costume designer, 1934

'She made Marilyn Monroe look like Shirley Temple.'
Humphrey Bogart, actor, on actress Gina Lollobrigida, attributed

'The body is meant to be seen, not all covered up.'
Marilyn Monroe, actress and voluptuous sex symbol

Youth

'In the costumes for *West Side Story* (1961) exaggeration and fantasy had no place . . . in the 1950s, the teenage boys on the streets of New York had arrived at a uniform of their own—not yet taken up as fashionable by men and women—consisting of blue jeans or chinos, T-shirts, windbreakers, and sneakers. It was an outfit economical and comfortable.'
Irene Sharaff, costume designer, 1976

'I have always felt Hollywood very instrumental in America's being so wildly youth conscious. It does become contagious—this trying to look years younger.'
Bette Davis, actress, 1908–89

'The secret of staying young is to live honestly, eat slowly and lie about your age.'
Lucille Ball, actress, comedienne and television star, 1911–89

Zips

Zipless designs were the result of Marilyn Monroe's predilection for being sewn into some of her more revealing dresses. One example was the 'nude' soufflé fabric beaded dress she asked costume designer Jean Louis to design for her (worn for her rendition of 'Happy Birthday' to President Kennedy in 1962), with the explicit instruction: 'Make this a dress only Marilyn Monroe can wear.'

'The gold lamé dress I made for Marilyn Monroe in *Gentlemen Prefer Blondes* (1953) was all done with two pieces of circular lamé wrapped on the body to a bias back seam. All the pleats measured exactly, there were no darts and no side seams. In fact it was so close-fitting, Marilyn had to be sewn into it . . . when Marilyn asked me for the dress [for the *Photoplay* Awards, where she won "Fastest Rising Star of 1952"], I told her she couldn't have it. It's a costume . . . so delicate it wouldn't take a zipper, we had to baste the back seam together by hand.'
William Travilla, costume designer, 1920–90

'The frustration caused by a stuck zip is indescribable. Learn to repair zips. You will save time, nerves and money.'
Marlene Dietrich, actress and singer, 1961

Zsa Zsa Gabor

'Zsa Zsa Gabor fits into no category whatsoever! She is a law unto herself! She is an institution. She represents feminity, love of diamonds, beauty, luxury. There is no question of her image. In fact, it even bears her name. I've heard people say, "You have so many diamonds you look like Zsa Zsa!" Zsa Zsa herself has made a career of looking like Zsa Zsa Gabor and she's not dreaming of changing that, she's very shrewd and intelligent.'
Edith Head, costume designer, 1974

'Zsa Zsa is unique. She's a woman from the court of Louis XV who has somehow managed to live in the twentieth century. She says she wants to be all the Pompadours and DuBarrys of history rolled into one.'
Gerold Frank, writer and biographer of Zsa Zsa Gabor, 1960

ACKNOWLEDGMENTS

Very appreciative thanks must go, first, to Mark Eastment, Head of V&A Publishing, and to Clare Faulkner in the marketing department of V&A Publishing, for giving me an excuse to delve into the fascinating realms of Hollywood style by inviting me to do this book, and many thanks are also due to the editor, Frances Ambler, and copy editor, Sarah Drinkwater, for their positive input and care in crafting this book.

I would like to thank Lauretta Dives, the incomparable Phil, Cheryl and everyone at the wonderful Kobal Collection, and Danielle Tamura at the marvellous Getty Images for their assistance with the picture research. Thanks also go to the knowledgeable staff at the British Film Institute library, and to Keara Stewart and the helpful staff at the London College of Fashion library. I would also like to pay tribute to the importance of the eight public libraries in Westminster, and Kensington and Chelsea, where I undertook necessary research, and particularly to Peter at the Westminster Reference Library.

Special thanks go to Tiffany Stemp and Sairey Stemp for their generous help and support; grateful thanks also to Tiffany Stemp for her constructive suggestions and improvements on reading my initial draft, which have undoubtedly made this a better book than it otherwise would have been.

'Few pleasures are greater than that of gazing at the stars—both those in the night sky and in our own man-made heavens of the theatre and the cinema.'
Colette, The American Weekly, 23 March 1952

How to Use This Book

The quotations in this book have been drawn from many sources, some famous, others widely circulated and repeated, and some obscure.

Where it has not been possible to date a quote exactly to a year, the dates of its author are given.

For further information, the following section is split into two. The first is organized by Hollywood star: it provides all the page numbers for quotations from a particular person, as well as further biographical information and the written source where appropriate. The second section provides details of other titles and articles from where quotes have been taken.

Details of the photographs used throughout the book are given on page 159.

REFERENCES

Mercedes de Acosta
American poet, writer and playwright, reputed to have had a long relationship with Greta Garbo (1893–1968): 116

Adrian
Born Adrian Adolph Greenberg.
Hollywood costume designer and fashion designer, made famous by the popular film credit 'Gowns by Adrian' (1903–59): 13, 15, 51, 66, 68, 72, 102
Gowns by Adrian: The MGM Years 1928–1941, Howard Gutner (New York, 2001): 29, 29, 32, 36, 36, 37, 67, 89, 103, 121

Ursula Andress
Swiss-born actress (1936–): 21

Eve Arnold
Born Eve Cohen.
American photojournalist and writer, best known for her images of Marilyn Monroe (1912–2012)
Marilyn Monroe: An Appreciation (New York, 1987, rev. 1989): 16, 71, 75, 91, 98, 129, 130

Fred Astaire
Born Frederick Austerlitz.
Hollywood actor, dancer, choreographer, singer and style icon (1899–1987): 19, 69
Steps in Time: An Autobiography (London, 1960): 114
Fred Astaire Style, G. Bruce Boyer (New York, 2004): 109, 119
Fred Astaire: His Friends Talk, Sarah Giles, ed. (London, 1988): 11, 12, 18, 103, 108, 109, 111, 114, 120
Astaire: The Biography, Tim Satchell (London, 1987): 9
'Fred Astaire: 1899–1987: The Great Flyer', Richard Schickel, *Time*, 6 July 1987: 42
Astaire: The Man, the Dancer, Bob Thomas (London, 1985): 112

Gene Autry
Born Orvon Grover Autry.
American singer-songwriter and actor, known as 'The Singing Cowboy' (1907–1998): 85

Lauren Bacall
Born Betty Joan Perske.
Hollywood actress and former model (1924–): 17
By Myself (New York, 1978): 60
Review of Lauren Bacall in *Sweet Bird of Youth*, Ros Asquith, *The Observer*, 14 July 1985: 58

Lucille Ball
Born Lucille Desirée Ball.
Hollywood actress, television star and comedienne (1911–89): 133
The Real Story of Lucille Ball, Eleanor Harris (New York, 1954): 114

Albert 'Cubby' Broccoli
Hollywood producer (1909–96)
When The Snow Melts: The Autobiography Of Cubby Broccoli, with Donald Zec (London, 1998): 97

Barbara Broccoli
Born Barbara Dana Broccoli.
Hollywood producer (1960–), daughter of producer 'Cubby' Broccoli: 21

Louise Brooks
Born Mary Louise Brooks.
Hollywood actress, dancer and writer (1906–85), famous as 'The Girl in the Black Helmet' for her sleek bobbed hairstyle, and the inspiration for Liza Minnelli's portrayal of Sally Bowles in *Cabaret* (1972): 18

Richard Burton
Welsh-born actor (1925–84): 23

Truman Capote
Born Truman Streckfus Persons.
American writer and author of the 1958 novella *Breakfast at Tiffany's* (1924–1984): 63, 121

Leslie Caron
Born Leslie Claire Margaret Caron.
French actress and dancer (1931–): 11, 73, 75, 103

Oleg Cassini
French-born fashion and costume designer who was married to Hollywood actress Gene Tierney and almost married actress Grace Kelly (1913–2006)
In My Own Fashion: An Autobiography (London, 1987): 42, 59, 119

Gabrielle 'Coco' Chanel
Paris-based French couturière and fashion designer (1883–1971)
Coco Chanel: A Biography, Axel Madsen (London, 1990): 32
The Allure of Chanel, Paul Morand (Paris, 1976): 19, 32, 33, 33

Winston Churchill
Born Winston Leonard Spencer-Churchill.
British politician and statesman, former Prime Minister, historian, writer and artist (1874–1965): 17

Montgomery Clift
Born Edward Montgomery Clift.
American actor and sex symbol (1920–66): 84

Claudette Colbert
French-born Hollywood actress (1903–96): 45, 78, 126

Joan Collins
British actress (1933–): 23, 61

Gary Cooper
Hollywood actor (1901–61)
Gary Cooper: Enduring Style, G. Bruce Boyer and Maria Cooper Janis (New York, 2011):
69, 109, 119, 130

Joan Crawford
Born Lucille Fay Le Sueur.
Hollywood actress and dancer (1905–77): 9, 15, 27, 35, 37, 51, 56, 58, 77, 85, 87, 100,
102, 104, 120, 121
A Portrait of Joan: The Autobiography of Joan Crawford, with Jane Kesner Ardmore
(London, 1963): 49, 69
Hollywood Martyr, David Bret (London, 2008): 81

George Cukor
Born George Dewey Cukor.
Hollywood director (1899–1983): 66, 85

Robert Cummings
Hollywood actor (1910–90): 93

Lilly Daché
French milliner, based in New York, designed for Hollywood and its stars (1898–1989)
Talking Through My Hats (New York, 1946): 41, 62

Bette Davis
Born Ruth Elizabeth Davis.
Hollywood film, stage and television actress (1908–89): 43, 75, 91, 106, 113, 133
This 'n That, with Michael Herskowitz (New York, 1987): 28
The Girl Who Walked Home Alone, Charlotte Chandler (London, 2006): 56, 81

Doris Day
Born Doris Mary Ann Kappelhoff.
Hollywood actress and singer (1924–)
Doris Day: Her Own Story, with A. E. Hotchner (New York, 1976): 127

Dolores del Río
Born María de los Dolores Asúnsolo López Negrete.
Mexican-born actress, beauty and style icon (1905–83): 16, 87, 117

Cecil B. DeMille
American film director and producer (1881–1959): 103

Cameron Diaz
Born Cameron Michelle Diaz.
Hollywood actress (1972–): 71

Angie Dickinson
Hollywood actress (1931–): 39

REFERENCES

Marlene Dietrich
Born Marie Magdalene Dietrich; Marlene was a conflation of her Christian and middle names.
German-born Hollywood actress, singer, cabaret artiste and style icon (1901–92): 11, 15, 30, 54, 71, 81, 87
Marlene Dietrich's ABC (New York, 1961): 39, 41, 47, 79, 81, 87, 93, 100, 134
My Life, Marlene Dietrich (London, 1989): 56, 99
'Felicity Green in Paris', Felicity Green, *Daily Mirror*, 5 August 1966: 11
'Me and My Clothes', Dietrich interviewed by Cynthia Kee, *The Observer*, 6 March 1960: 107
Marlene Dietrich, Maria Riva (London, 1992): 45, 77, 105, 116
'Marlene Dietrich Tells Why She Wears Men's Clothes!', Rosalind Shaffer, *Motion Picture*, vol. 45, issue 3, 1933: 11, 11, 116

Simon Doonan
British-born window dresser extraordinaire, writer and Creative Ambassador-at-Large of American designer clothing store group Barneys (1952–): 113

Faye Dunaway
Born Dorothy Faye Dunaway.
Hollywood actress (1941–): 25
Looking for Gatsby: My Life, with Betsey Sharkey (London, 1995): 20, 49, 62, 97, 105
Film Yearbook 1989 (New York, 1988)

Allan Dwan
Canadian-born Hollywood director, producer and screenwriter (1885–1981): 57

Luis Estevez
Cuban-born fashion and costume designer (1930–): 24

Max Factor
Born Maksymilian Faktorowicz.
Polish-born cosmetician (1877–1938)
Max Factor: The Man Who Changed the Faces of the World, Fred E. Basten (New York, 2008): 43

Carrie Fisher
Born Carrie Frances Fisher.
Hollywood actress and writer (1956–): 26

Errol Flynn
Tasmanian-born Hollywood actor (1909–59)
Errol Flynn: The Life and Career, Thomas McNulty (North Carolina, 2004): 85, 107

Eva Gabor
Hungarian-born Hollywood actress (1919–95): 9, 119

Zsa Zsa Gabor
Born Sári Gábor.
Hungarian-born Hollywood actress (1917–)
Zsa Zsa Gabor, My Story: 72

Clark Gable
Born William Clark Gable.
Hollywood actor (1901–60)
Coronet Magazine, February 1961: 66, 123

Greta Garbo
Born Greta Lovisa Gustafsson; 'Garbo' is Swedish for 'wood nymph,' and Spanish for 'grace.'
Swedish-born Hollywood actress and style icon (1905–90): 12, 35, 37
Conversations with Garbo, Sven Broman (New York, 1991): 35
The Divine Garbo, Frederick Sands and Sven Broman (London, 1979): 99
'The Garbo Image,' Parker Tyler in *The Films of Garbo*, M. Conway, D. McGregor, M. Ricci, eds. (New York, 1963): 13, 43, 58, 66
Loving Garbo, Hugo Vickers (London, 1994): 116

Ava Gardner
Born Ava Lavinia Gardner.
Hollywood actress and famed beauty (1922–90): 107

Judy Garland
Born Frances Ethel Gumm.
Hollywood actress and singer (1922–69): 65

Terry Gilliam
American-born screenwriter, director, animator, actor and member of British comedy group Monty Python (1940–): 123

Hubert de Givenchy
Born Count Hubert James Marcel Taffin de Givenchy.
French couturier, costume designer and consultant to Audrey Hepburn on many of her films (1927–)
The Givenchy Style, Francoise Mohrt (New York, 1998): 108

Elinor Glyn
Born Elinor Sutherland.
British novelist, screenwriter and director (1864–1943): 69

Sam Goldwyn, Jr.
Hollywood film producer, son of pioneering film mogul Sam Goldwyn (1926–): 103

Cary Grant
Born Archibald Alexander Leach.
British-born Hollywood actor (1904–86): 35, 42, 77, 84, 93, 100, 103, 110
'Archie Leach': An Autobiography (*Ladies Home Journal*, 1963, http://archieleach.com): 103
The Private Cary Grant, William Currie McIntosh and William D. Weaver (London, revd. 1987): 9, 59
'Cary Grant: The Man From Dream City', Pauline Kael, *The New Yorker*, 14 July 1975: 9, 10, 113
Cary Grant: A Class Apart, Graham McCann (London, 1996): 10, 113

'Cary Grant's Suit,' Todd McEwen, *Granta*, issue 94, summer 2006: 109
Cary Grant: A Portrait in His Own Words and By Those Who Knew Him Best, Nancy Nelson (London, 1991)
Cary Grant: A Celebration of Style, Richard Torregrossa (London, 2006): 25, 58, 110, 110

Howard Greer
Hollywood costume designer and fashion designer (1896–1974)
Designing Male (New York, 1949): 32, 68, 127

Mack Grey
Hollywood actor (1905–81): 53

Jean Harlow
Born Harlean Harlow Carpenter.
Hollywood actress and the original platinum blonde (1911–37): 19, 35, 87, 91, 93, 120, 123

Julie Harris
British costume designer (1921–)
'Style: The Screen's Most Glamorous,' *The Hollywood Reporter*, 16 December 2010: 47

Rita Hayworth
Born Margarita Carmen Cansino.
Hollywood actress and dancer (1918–87)
The Films of Rita Hayworth: The Legend and Career of a Love Goddess, Gene Ringgold (New Jersey, 1975): 85
Rita Hayworth: The Time, the Place and the Woman, John Kobal (London, 1977): 61

Edith Head
Hollywood costume designer, television presenter and writer (1897–1981): 19, 27, 29, 30, 37, 49, 119
The Dress Doctor, with Jane Ardmore (Surrey, 1959): 13, 27, 28, 29, 30, 35, 36, 41, 45, 62, 73, 77, 78, 87, 102, 113
Edith Head's Hollywood, Paddy Calistro (New York, 1983): 20, 30, 51, 57, 58, 59, 84, 95, 106, 107, 115, 121, 126
Edith Head: The Life and Times of Hollywood's Celebrated Costume Designer, David Chierichetti (New York, 2004): 103, 124
Edith Head, The Fifty-Year Career of Hollywood's Greatest Costume Designer, Jay Jorgensen (Philadelphia, 2010): 88
Hollywood Speaks! An Oral History, Mike Steen (New York, 1974): 121, 134

Audrey Hepburn
Born Audrey Ruston-Hepburn.
Belgian-born Hollywood actress, style icon, and UNICEF ambassador (1929–93): 119
'Audrey, Darling,' Lesley Caron, British *Vogue*, April 1993: 73, 75, 103
Audrey Style, Pamela Clarke Keogh (New York, 1999): 17, 107
'The Costumes Make the Actors: A Personal View,' *Fashion in Film*, Regine Engelmeier and Peter Engelmeier, eds. (Munich, 1990): 28, 62
'Woman of our Dreams,' Deirdre Fernand in *Audrey Hepburn in Breakfast at Tiffany's*

and other Photos (Munich, 2003): 103
The Audrey Hepburn Way of Life: How to be Lovely, Melissa Hellstern (London, 2008): 93, 119
Audrey Hepburn, An Elegant Spirit, Sean Hepburn Ferrer (London 2003): 139
Audrey Hepburn: The Paramount Years, Tony Nourmand (London, 2006): 65, 119
Audrey Hepburn, Barry Paris (London, 1997): 30, 126

Katharine Hepburn
Born Katharine Houghton Hepburn.
Hollywood actress (1907–2003)
Kate: The Woman Who Was Katharine Hepburn, William J. Mann (London, 2006): 117

Alfred Hitchcock
British director and producer (1899–1980): 27, 84, 97, 98, 107, 123, 124, 126
Hitchcock on Hitchcock: Selected Writings and Interviews, Sidney Gottlieb, ed. (London, 1997): 21, 41
Spellbound by Beauty: Alfred Hitchcock and his Leading Ladies, Donald Spoto (London, 2008)

Hedda Hopper
Born Elda Flurry.
Hollywood gossip columnist and actress (1885–1966)
The Whole Truth and Nothing But (New York, 1963): 56

Barbara Hulanicki
Polish-born illustrator, fashion designer, boutique owner, entrepreneur and interior designer (1936–)
From A to Biba (London, 1983): 48, 79

George Hurrell
Hollywood photographer, principally known for his stills portraits of Hollywood stars (1904–92)
People Will Talk, John Kobal (London, 1986): 54, 56

John Huston
American director, screenwriter and actor (1906–87): 89

Jean Louis
Born Jean Louis Berthault.
French-born Hollywood costume designer, especially known for Marlene Dietrich's cabaret outfits and for his designs for Rita Hayworth, Marilyn Monroe and Doris Day (1907–97): 79, 95, 98

Ray Jones
American photographer (1900–75): 54

Robert Kalloch
Hollywood costume designer (1893–1947): 133

Gene Kelly
Born Eugene Curran Kelly.
Hollywood dancer, choreographer, singer, director and producer (1912–96)
Gene Kelly: A Biography, Clive Hirschhorn (London, 1984): 108, 114

Grace Kelly
Hollywood actress, later Her Serene Highness Princess Grace of Monaco (1929–82): 9
Princess Grace, Gwen Robyns (New York, 1978): 57
High Society: Grace Kelly and Hollywood, Donald Spoto (London, 2009): 59

Nancy 'Slim' Keith, Lady Keith
Born Nancy Gross.
American socialite and style icon of the 1950s and '60s (1917–90): 18

Calvin Klein
Born Calvin Richard Klein.
American fashion designer (1942–): 117

John Kobal
Born Ivan Kobaly.
Film historian, writer and founder of The Kobal Collection (1940–91)
Movie-Star Portraits of the Forties (New York, 1977): 85
People Will Talk (London, 1986): 26, 54, 61, 68, 107, 129

Veronica Lake
Born Constance Frances Marie Ockelman.
Hollywood actress (1922–73)
Veronica (London, 1969): 91, 114

Hedy Lamarr
Born Hedwig Kiesler.
Austrian-born Hollywood actress, hailed by Louis B. Mayer as 'The Most Beautiful Woman in Film.' Lamarr's 'feline beauty' and svelte figure inspired Bob Kane's 1940 comic book creation Cat, later Catwoman. Invented, with composer George Antheil, a secret weapons communications system for use during WWII; though rejected by the U.S. Navy, her invention is widely used today, forming the basis of wifi and cordless and wireless phone technology. (1914–2000): 104
Hedy Lamarr: The Most Beautiful Woman in Film, Ruth Barton (Kentucky, 2010): 54, 72

Dorothy Lamour
Born Mary Leta Dorothy Slaton.
Hollywood actress (1914–96): 54

Bernard Lansky
Owner of a high-fashion menswear store and tailors in Memphis, Lansky, dubbed 'clothier to the King,' supplied Elvis Presley with much of his wardrobe, including his first suit (1927–2012): 111

James Laver
British art and fashion historian, writer and V&A curator (1899–1975): 6, 16

Lucien Lelong
Parisian couturier (1889–1958): 32

Carole Lombard
Hollywood actress (1908–42): 82

Bob Mackie
Born Robert Gordon Mackie.
Fashion and costume designer, famous for his flamboyant and exhibitionist designs for the singer and actress Cher, and for other entertainment divas (1940–): 89, 114, 120

John Malkovich
Hollywood actor, producer, director, fashion designer (1953–): 37

Joseph L. Mankiewicz
Born Joseph Leo Mankiewicz.
Hollywood director, screenwriter and producer (1909–93): 104

Anthony Mann
Hollywood actor and director (1906–97): 130

Jayne Mansfield
Born Vera Jayne Palmer.
Hollywood actress (1933–67): 27, 100, 127

Roddy McDowell
Born Roderick Andrew Anthony Jude McDowell.
Hollywood actor and photographer (1928–98): 43

Alexander McQueen
Born Lee Alexander McQueen.
British fashion designer (1969–2010): 109

Liza Minnelli
Born Liza May Minnelli.
American singer and actress, daughter of singer and actress Judy Garland and director Vincente Minnelli (1946–): 11, 109

Robert Mitchum
Born Roger Charles Durman Mitchum.
Hollywood actor (1917–97): 84

Isaac Mizrahi
American fashion designer (1961–)
Secrets of Stylists: An Insider's Guide to Styling the Stars, Sasha Chernin Morrison (New York, 2011): 48

Marilyn Monroe
Born Norma Jeane Mortenson.
Hollywood actress and legendary style icon (1926–62): 13, 21, 23, 59, 71, 82, 99, 119,

120, 133

Foreword, *Glamour: Film Fashion and Beauty*, Peter Noble and Yvonne Saxon, eds. (London, 1953): 82

'Marilyn Monroe: My Beauty Secrets,' *Photoplay*, October 1953: 59

'A Beautiful Child,' Truman Capote, 1955, reprinted in *Music for Chameleons* (New York, 1980): 121

'Before the Literary Bar,' Norman Mailer, *New York Magazine*, 10 November 1980: 41

Marilyn, Hitler and Me, Milton Shulman (Michigan, 1998): 98

Monroe: Her Life in Pictures, James Spada with George Zeno (London, 1982): 20, 26, 91

Roger Moore
Born Roger George Moore.
British actor and UNICEF Goodwill Ambassador (1927–): 17

Vinicius de Moraes
Brazilian poet, composer, playwright and diplomat (1913–1980): 126

Deborah Nadoolman Landis
Costume designer and writer on Hollywood costume design
Costume Design (Burlington, MA, 2003): 125
Dressed: A Century of Hollywood Costume Design (New York, 2007): 57, 130

Marshall Ambrose Neilan
Hollywood actor, screenwriter, director and producer (1891–1958): 106

Jack Nicholson
Hollywood actor, director and producer (1937–): 111

Merle Oberon
Indian-born British actress and beauty (1911–79): 15

Orry-Kelly
Born Orry George Kelly.
Australian-born Hollywood costume designer (1897–1964): 30

Jack Paar
American author, comedian and talk-show host (1918–2004): 87

Al Pacino
Hollywood actor and director (1940–): 124

Gwyneth Paltrow
Born Gwyneth Kate Paltrow.
Hollywood actress and lifestyle entrepreneur (1972–): 18

Hermes Pan
Born Hermes Panagiotopoulos.
Hollywood dancer and choreographer, collaborated with his friend Fred Astaire (1910–90): 12

Cecilia Parker
Canadian-born Hollywood actress (1914–93): 58

Gregory Peck
Born Eldred Gregory Peck.
Hollywood actor (1916–2003): 107

Walter Plunkett
Hollywood costume designer (1902–82): 88, 100

Paul Poiret
Parisian couturier (1879–1944): 32

Anthony Powell
British costume designer (1935–): 124

Jane Powell
Born Suzanne Lorraine Bruce.
Hollywood actress (1929–): 77

Ginger Rogers
Born Virginia Katherine McMath.
Hollywood actress, dancer and singer (1911–95)
Ginger: My Story (London, 1991): 27

Isabella Rossellini
Born Isabella Fiorella Elettra Giovanna Rossellini.
Hollywood actress, filmmaker, philanthropist and former model; daughter of Hollywood
actress Ingrid Bergman (1952–): 17

Helena Rubinstein
Born Chaja Rubinstein.
Polish-born founder of eponymous cosmetics empire (1870–1965): 81

Jane Russell
Born Ernestine Jane Geraldine Russell.
Hollywood actress (1921–2011)
Jane Russell: An Autobiography (London, 1986): 78

Eva Marie Saint
Hollywood actress (1924–): 25, 102, 109, 110

Yves Saint Laurent
Algerian-born couturier and fashion designer, based in Paris (1936–2008)

Elsa Schiaparelli
Italian-born, Paris-based couturiere and fashion designer (1890–1973): 25, 33
Shocking Life (London, 1954): 102
Elsa Schiaparelli: Empress of Paris Fashion, Palmer White (London, 1986): 32

David O. Selznick
Hollywood film producer (1902–65): 48

Irene Sharaff
Hollywood costume designer (1910–93)
Broadway and Hollywood Costumes Design (London, 1976): 23, 26, 133
The New York Times, 17 August 1993: 108

Norma Shearer
Born Edith Norma Shearer.
Hollywood actress (1902–83): 37, 57

Ann Sheridan
Hollywood actress (1915–67): 85

Vincent Sherman
American director and actor (1906–2006): 107

Frank Sinatra
Born Francis Albert Sinatra.
Legendary American singer and Hollywood actor, known as 'Ol' Blue Eyes,' married four
times, twice to Hollywood actresses: Ava Gardner (1951–7) and Mia Farrow (1966–8),
(1915–98): 63, 100, 126

Allan 'Whitey' Snyder
Hollywood makeup artist, and Marilyn Monroe's personal makeup artist (1914–94): 82

Ginette Spanier
Directrice at the couture House of Balmain, Paris
It Isn't All Mink (London, 1959): 77

Steven Spielberg
Hollywood director, screenwriter, producer and film entrepreneur (1946–): 24

Robert Stack
Born Robert Langford Modini Stack.
Hollywood actor (1919–2003): 116

Barbara Stanwyck
Born Ruby Catherine Steven.
Hollywood actress (1907–90): 124

Tommy Steele
Born Thomas William Hicks.
British singer and actor (1936–): 108

James Stewart
Hollywood actor (1908–97): 39, 130
Film Yearbook 1990 (New York, 1989): 90

Sharon Stone
Born Sharon Vonne Stone.
Hollywood actress, producer and former model (1958–): 10

Barbra Streisand
Singer and Hollywood actress, director and producer (1942–): 17

Gloria Swanson
Born Gloria Josephine Mae Swanson.
Hollywood actress (1899–1983): 57
Swanson on Swanson (New York, 1980): 72, 79, 106, 129

Quentin Tarantino
Born Quentin Jerome Tarantino.
Hollywood director, producer, actor and screenwriter (1963–): 29

Elizabeth Taylor
Born Elizabeth Rosemond Taylor.
British-born Hollywood actress and charity campaigner (1932–2011): 23, 73, 124, 129
'A Lustrous Pinnacle of Hollywood Glamour,' Mel Gussow, *The New York Times*, 23 March 2011: 65, 127
'An Alluring Beauty Exempt from Fashion's Rules,' Cathy Horyn, *The New York Times*, 23 March 2011: 108

Spencer Tracy
Born Spencer Bonaventure Tracy.
Hollywood actor who had a long-term on- and off-screen relationship with actress Katharine Hepburn (1900–67): 117

William Travilla
Hollywood costume designer who dubbed himself the 'King of Cleavage' (1920–90)
Hollywood Costume Design by Travilla, Maureen Reilly (Atglen, PA, 2003): 20, 85, 134

Lana Turner
Born Julia Jean Turner.
Hollywood actress (1921–95): 25, 56, 82

Valentino
Italian couturier and fashion designer (1932–)
Valentino: A Grand Italian Epic, Armando Chitolina, ed. (New York, 2009): 30, 35, 48

Mamie Van Doren
Hollywood actress (1931–): 21

Theadora Van Runkle
Hollywood costume designer (1928–2011): 29, 71

Diana Vreeland
Fashion editor, American *Harper's Bazaar* 1937–62: editor-in-chief, American *Vogue*

1963–71; and consultant/curator for the Costume Institute at the Metropolitan Museum of Art, New York, 1972–89 (1903–89)
Romantic and Glamorous Hollywood Design, Dale McConathy and Diana Vreeland (New York, 1976): 79, 103
DV (London, 1984): 10

Jerry Wald
Hollywood producer and screenwriter (1911–62): 58

John Wayne
Born Marion Robert Morrison.
Hollywood actor, director and producer (1907–79): 130

Sigourney Weaver
Born Susan Alexandra Weaver.
Hollywood actress (1949–): 49

Mae West
Born Mary Jane West.
Hollywood actress, playwright and screenwriter, and wit (1893–1980): 13, 26, 35, 37, 63, 72, 73, 98, 104, 117, 127, 129
Goodness Had Nothing to Do with It (New Jersey, 1959): 73
She Always Knew How: Mae West, a Personal Biography, Charlotte Chandler (New York, 2009): 9, 16
Hollywood: Legend and Reality, Michael Webb (Boston, 1986): 57
Attitude: Hats, Pure Hulton Getty (London, 1999): 69

Audrey Wilder
Born Audrey Young.
American singer and actress, married to Hollywood director Billy Wilder (1949–2002): 93

Billy Wilder
Hollywood director, producer and screenwriter (1906–2002)
Conversations with Wilder, Cameron Crowe (New York, 1999): 20, 26, 108, 129

Tennessee Williams
American writer and playwright (1911–83): 10, 75

Shelley Winters
Hollywood actress (1920–2006): 130
The Sunday Express, 12 January 1975: 81

Natalie Wood
Born Natalia Nikolaevna Zakharenko.
Hollywood actress (1938–81): 93

Albert Wolsky
Hollywood costume designer (1930–): 41, 93

Loretta Young
Hollywood actress (1913–2000): 15, 37, 56

Catherine Zeta-Jones
Welsh-born Hollywood actress, married to fellow actor Michael Douglas (1969–): 82

QUOTES ARE ALSO TAKEN FROM:

Sally Alexander, 'Becoming a Woman in London in the 1920s and 1930s' in D. Feldman and G.S. Jones, eds., *Metropolis: Histories and Representations of London since 1800* (London, 1989): 68

James Bacon, *Made in Hollywood* (Chicago, 1977): 35

Margaret Bailey, *Those Glorious Glamour Years: Classic Hollywood Costume Designs of the 1930s* (New Jersey, 1982): 13, 15, 30, 36, 46, 57, 133

Mark Bego, *The Best of Modern Screen* (London, 1986): 9, 27, 37, 87, 100, 120, 123

Stella Bruzzi, *Undressing Cinema: Clothing and Identity in the Movies* (London, 1997): 53

Gerda Buxbaum, *Icons of Fashion*, rev. ed. (London, 2005): 66

Charlotte Chandler, *The Ultimate Seduction* (New York, 1984): 65, 124

David Chierichetti, *Hollywood Costume Design* (London, 1976): 100

John Cork and Maryam D'Abo, *Bond Girls Are Forever: The Women of James Bond* (London, 2003): 21

Ronald L. Davis, *The Glamour Factory: Inside Hollywood's Big Studio System* (Dallas, 1993): 48, 49, 77

Nicholas Drake, *The Fifties in Vogue* (London, 1987): 17

John Fairchild, *The Fashionable Savages* (New York, 1965): 18, 24, 47, 63, 69, 106

Herbert Farjeon, British *Vogue*, 22 March 1933: 67

Nick Foulkes, *The Trench Book* (New York, 2007): 115, 116

Patty Fox, *Star Style at the Academy Awards: A Century of Glamour* (Santa Monica, 2000): 89, 109, 117

Patty Fox, *Star Style: Hollywood Legends as Fashion Icons* (Santa Monica, 1995): 13, 24, 58, 82, 117

Philip French, *Movie Moguls: An Informal History of the Hollywood Tycoons* (London, 1969): 113

Prudence Glynn, *In Fashion: Dress in the Twentieth Century* (London, 1978): 95

Leslie Halliwell, *The Filmgoer's Book of Quotes* (London, 1973): 99

Anne Hollander, *Seeing Through Clothes* (New York, 1978): 45

Georgina Howell, *In Vogue: 75 Years of Style* (London, 1991): 6, 16

Pauline Kael, 'Cary Grant: The Man From Dream City,' *The New Yorker*, 14 July 1975: 9, 10, 113, 133

Brigid Keenan, *The Women We Wanted To Look Like* (London, 1977): 81

Pamela Klaffke, *Spree: A Cultural History of Shopping* (Vancouver, 2003): 124

Robert LaVine, *In a Glamorous Fashion: The Fabulous Years of Hollywood Costume Design* (London, 1980): 68, 72, 79, 91

Elizabeth Leese, *Costume Design in the Movies: An Illustrated Guide to the Work of 157 Great Designers* (New York, 1991)

Tony Macklin and Nick Pici, eds., *Voices from the Set: The Film Heritage Interviews* (London, 2000): 19, 130

Edward Maeder, ed., *Hollywood and History: Costume Design in Film* (London, 1987): 32

Arthur Marwick, *Beauty in History* (London, 1988): 17

Ellen Melinkoff, *What We Wore* (New York, 1984): 79

Joe Morella and Edward Z. Epstein, *Paulette: The Adventurous Life of Paulette Goddard* (New York, 1985)

Glenn O'Brien, *The Style Guy* (New York, 2000): 25

Camille Paglia, 'Paglia on Taylor: "A luscious, opulent, ripe fruit,"' Salon.com, 24 March 2011, www.Salon.com/2011/03/24camille_paglia_on_elizabeth_taylor: 126

Joanna Pitman, *On Blondes: From Aphrodite to Madonna: Why Blondes Have More Fun* (London, 2004): 75

Penny Proddow and Debra Healy, *Hollywood Jewels: Movies, Jewelry, Stars* (New York, 1992): 72

Margaret Reid, 'Has the Flapper Changed? F. Scott Fitzgerald Discusses the Cinema Descendants of the Type He has Made So Well Known,' *Motion Picture Magazine*, July 1927: 51, 51

Julian Robinson, *Fashion in the Thirties* (London, 1978): 33

William A. Rossi, *The Sex Life of the Foot and Shoe* (Ware, Herts., 1977): 99, 100

Alexandria Sage, 'Risky revealing gowns catch Oscar's eye,' *Washington Post*, 30 January 2007

Dorothy Schefer, *What is Beauty? New Definitions from the Fashion Vanguard* (London, 1997): 17

Sandy Schreier, *Hollywood Dressed and Undressed: A Century of Cinema Style* (New York, 1998): 84, 109, 113

Robin Langley Sommer, *Hollywood: The Glamour Years, 1919–1941* (New York, 1987): 81

Annette Tapert, *The Power of Glamour: The Women Who Defined the Magic of Stardom* (New York, 1998): 11, 12, 13, 15, 16, 45, 56, 71, 78, 87, 104, 117, 126

Paul Trent, *The Image Makers: Sixty Years of Hollywood Glamour* (London, 1972): 56, 102, 121

Kenneth Tynan, *Show People: Profiles in Entertainment* (London, 1989): 10, 12, 53, 53, 61

Simone Werle, *Fashionisto: A Century of Fashion Icons* (London, 2010): 100, 111

Elizabeth Wilson, 'Audrey Hepburn: fashion, film and the '50s,' in Pam Cook and Philip Dodd, eds., *Women and Film: A Sight and Sound Reader* (London, 1993, reprinted 1997): 49, 53

'The Fashion Industry Bumps into Hollywood,' *Click Magazine*, 1938, http://www.oldmagazinearticles.com/Fashion_1930s: 68

'*GQ*'s Top 25 Films That Have Influenced Men's Fashions over the Past 50 Years', *GQ*, October 2006: 110

'The 50 Most Stylish Leading Men of the Past Half Century,' *GQ*, March 2010: 58, 107

IMAGE CREDITS

p.5 Carole Lombard, *c.*1935. John Kobal Foundation/Getty Images; **p.8** Greta Garbo, 1932. Apic/Hulton Archive/Getty Images; **p.14** Grace Kelly, *c.*1955. Archive Photos/Stringer/Getty Images; **p.15** Dolores del Río, 1932. The Kobal Collection/John Miehle; **p.19** Jean Harlow, date unknown. The Kobal Collection/Elmer Fryer; **p.21** Ursula Andress, 1962. DANJAQ/EON/UA/The Kobal Collection; **p.22** Steve McQueen, 1968. Warner Bros/The Kobal Collection; **p.24** Clark Gable and Joan Crawford, 1936. MGM/The Kobal Collection/George Hurrell; **p.26** Elizabeth Taylor, undated. The Kobal Collection; **p.31** Grace Kelly, 1954. Paramount/The Kobal Collection; **p.33** Errol Flynn, 1935. Warner Bros/The Kobal Collection; **p.34** Dolores del Río, 1935. Warner Bros/The Kobal Collection; **p.36** Elizabeth Taylor, 1963. Keystone/Stringer/Getty Images; **p.38** Deborah Kerr, 1953. AFP/Stringer/Getty Images; **p.39** Marlene Dietrich, *c.*1934. Movie Pix/Getty Images/William Walling; **p.40** Katharine Hepburn, 1940. MGM/The Kobal Collection/Clarence Sinclair Bull; **p.42** Joan Crawford, 1956. Columbia/The Kobal Collection/ Bob Coburn; **p.43** Greta Garbo, 1931. MGM/The Kobal Collection; **p.44** Jean Harlow, 1934. MGM/The Kobal Collection/Harvey White; **p.46** Dovima and Audrey Hepburn, 1956. Paramount/The Kobal Collection; **p.50** Marlene Dietrich, 1930. GAB Archive/Getty Images; **p.52** Audrey Hepburn, *c.*1954. Getty Images/Bob Thomas; **p.55** Dorothy Lamour, 1936. Hulton Archive/Getty Images; **p.59** Grace Kelly, 1955. Paramount/The Kobal Collection; **p.60** Lauren Bacall, 1946. Warner Bros/The Kobal Collection/Scotty Welbourne; **p.61** Veronica Lake, 1944. Paramount/The Kobal Collection; **p.62** Carmen Miranda, *c.*1940. Michael Ochs Archives/Getty Images; **p.64** Clara Bow, 1926. Paramount/The Kobal Collection/E.R. Richee; **p.65** Marilyn Monroe, 1953. 20th Century Fox/The Kobal Collection/Frank Powolny; **p.70** James Dean, 1955. Warner Bros/The Kobal Collection; **p.73** Elizabeth Taylor, 1963. MGM/The Kobal Collection; **p.74** Mamie Van Doren, 1958. The Kobal Collection; **p.75** Faye Dunaway, 1967. Warner Bros/The Kobal Collection; **p.76** Audrey Hepburn, 1961. Hulton Archive/Stringer/Getty Images; **p.78** Audrey Hepburn, 1961. Keystone Features/Stringer/Getty Images; **p.80** Marlene Dietrich, 1941. Warner Bros/The Kobal Collection; **p.83** Cary Grant and Alfred Hitchcock, 1959. MGM/The Kobal Collection; **p.86** Rita Hayworth, 1941. Columbia/The Kobal Collection; **p.88** Edith Head, *c.*1955. Hulton Archive/Stringer/Getty Images; **p.90** Jean Harlow, 1933. MGM/The Kobal Collection/George Hurrell; **p.92** James Dean, 1955. Michael Ochs Archive/Getty Images; **p.94** Marlon Brando, 1953. Columbia/The Kobal Collection; **p.95** Jean Harlow, 1934. MGM/The Kobal Collection; **p.96** Gary Cooper, 1934. Paramount/The Kobal Collection/Clarence Sinclair Bull; **p.101** Joan Crawford, 1940. Hulton Archive/Getty Images; **p.105** Joan Crawford, 1933. MGM/The Kobal Collection/George Hurrell; **p.110** Cary Grant and Eva Maria Saint, 1959. MGM/The Kobal Collection; **p.112** Fred Astaire, 1948. MGM/The Kobal Collection/Clarence Sinclair Bull; **p.115** Humphrey Bogart, 1951. Columbia/The Kobal Collection; **p.117** Katharine Hepburn, 1938. Time & Life Pictures/Getty Images/Alfred Eisenstaedt; **p.118** Marlon Brando, 1951. Warner Bros/The Kobal Collection; **p.122** Louise Brooks, 1928. Paramount/The Kobal Collection/E.R. Richee; **p.125** Ruldolph Valentino, 1925. Getty Images; **p.127** Mae West, 1937. Hulton Archive/Stringer/Getty Images; **p.128** Marilyn Monroe, 1955. 20th Century Fox/The Kobal Collection; **p.131** Robert Redford, Katharine Ross and Paul Newman, 1969. 20th Century Fox/The Kobal Collection; **p.132** George Chakiris, 1961. Popperfoto/Getty Images; **p.135** Marilyn Monroe, 1953. 20th Century Fox/The Kobal Collection; **p.136** Faye Dunaway, 1977. Getty Images/Terry O'Neill; **p.138** Natalie Wood and Warren Beatty, 1961. New York Daily News Archive/Getty Images; **Endpapers** Press photographers in Paris, 1934. Hulton Archive/Getty Images